Basic Skills for the
TOEFL® iBT

Jeff Zeter

Compass
Publishing

Writing

1

Basic Skills for the TOEFL® iBT 1
Writing

Jeff Zeter

© 2008 Compass Publishing

Project Editor: Liana Robinson
Acquisitions Editor: Emily Page
Content Editor: Caroline Murphy
Copy Editor: Michael Jones
Contributing Writers: David Charlton, Moraig Macgillivray
Consultants: Lucy Han, Chanhee Park
Cover/Interior Design: Dammora Inc.

email: info@compasspub.com
http://www.compasspub.com

ISBN: 978-1-59966-154-4

10 9 8 7 6 5
10 09

Contents

Introduction to the TOEFL® iBT

What is the TOEFL® test?

The TOEFL® iBT (Test of English as a Foreign Language Internet-based Test) is designed to assess English proficiency in non-native speakers who want to achieve academic success as well as effective communication. It is not meant to test academic knowledge or computer ability; therefore, questions are always based on material found in the test.

The TOEFL® iBT test is divided into four sections:
- Reading
- Speaking
- Listening
- Writing

TOEFL® Scores

TOEFL® scores can be used for:
- Admission into university or college where instruction is in English
- Employers or government agencies who need to determine a person's English ability
- English-learning institutes that need to place students in the appropriate level of English instruction

It is estimated that about 4,400 universities and other institutions require a certain TOEFL® test score for admission.

The exact calculation of a TOEFL® test score is complicated and not necessary for the student to understand. However, it is helpful to know that:
- Each section in the Internet-based test is worth 30 points
- The highest possible score on the iBT is 120 points
- Each institution will have its own specific score requirements

✱ It is very important to check with each institution individually to find out what its admission requirements are.

Registering for the TOEFL® iBT

Students who wish to take the TOEFL® test must get registration information. Registration information can be obtained online at the ETS website. The Internet address is www.ets.org/toefl.

The website provides information such as:
- testing locations
- identification requirements
- registration information
- costs
- other test preparation material
- test center locations

This information will vary depending on the country in which you take the test. Be sure to follow the requirements carefully. If you do not have the proper requirements in order, you may not be able to take the test. Remember that if you register online, you will need to have your credit card information ready.

Introduction to the Writing Section of the TOEFL® iBT

The writing section of the test is designed to assess your ability to organize and support your ideas in essay format and use English correctly. You will have two writing tasks. One task is based both on a reading and on a lecture. You will be required to summarize the information you have heard and to relate the information heard in the lecture to the information in the passage. This is called Integrated Writing. The second task requires you to generate an essay based on your own experience. You will be given no material to work with; it will be based completely on your own ideas. This is called Independent Writing.

Question Types

Questions for the writing section of the TOEFL® iBT will appear in the following order:

Question	Type	Time	Response Length	Description
1	Integrated: 250-300 word reading 250-300 word lecture	20 minutes	150-225 words	Compare or contrast information presented in the reading passage with information presented in the lecture
2	Independent	30 minutes	300+ words	Present a personal opinion or describe an experience, including details and examples

How Writing Will Be Scored

ETS graders will score test takers' essays for writing tasks according to the following scale:

Score	General Description	Key Points
5	The **integrated** essay includes important information from both the reading and the lecture and appropriately explains the information with regard to the prompt. The **independent** essay answers the question well and the ideas are fully developed.	The essay is easy to understand and is well organized. There is good use of language, correct choice of words, and idioms to express ideas. Minor errors in grammar and word choice are acceptable.
4	The **integrated** essay includes most of the key points from the reading and the lecture as they relate to the prompt, but not all of the points are fully explained. The **independent** essay can be understood and answers the question, but not all of the ideas are fully developed.	There is good use of language, including an appropriate range of sentence structure and vocabulary. There are several minor errors with language, or some ideas may not seem connected, but these errors do not make comprehension difficult.
3	The **integrated** essay does not include or correctly explain a key point from the lecture or reading, or shows only a limited understanding of the information. The **independent** essay gives a basic answer to the question, but not many examples or details are provided.	Errors in sentence structure, grammar, and word choice may make the meaning of some sentences vague or difficult to comprehend. Transitions or connections between ideas are not always easy to follow. However, the important ideas in the essay can be understood.
2	The **integrated** essay does not include sufficient information from the reading, lecture, or both and the reader cannot follow connections between ideas. The **independent** essay is very short and not well organized. The ideas are not connected and examples are not explained.	Errors in sentence structure, grammar, and word choice appear in almost every sentence and make ideas in the essay difficult to understand in key points; readers unfamiliar with the reading and lecture/prompt may not be able to follow the essay.
1	The **integrated** essay includes few or none of the key points. The essay is poorly written and difficult to understand. The **independent** essay is short and confusing. Little or no detail is given to support ideas, and irrelevant information is included.	Frequent and serious errors in grammar and word choice make sentences in the essay impossible to understand.
0	The essay only copies words from the prompt or is not related to the topic at all.	Not enough of the student's writing is available to score

Test Management

- Before you begin the writing section, listen to the headset directions. It is very important that you can hear clearly during the lectures.

- Note-taking is permitted. Paper will be provided by the test supervisor. These notes can be studied when preparing your response.

- If you miss something that is said in a lecture, do not panic. Forget about it and simply keep listening. Even native speakers do not hear everything that is said.

- The reading passage disappears while listening and reappears after listening, so don't worry about taking notes on all of the key points in the reading. You will NOT be able to hear the listening again, so it is very important to take good notes while you listen.

- You have to type in your answers. You can use icon buttons at the top of the screen for editing. The editing tools include copy, cut, and paste.

- Keep the style of essay writing in English in mind. First, select a main idea, explain it clearly, then support and develop it using details and/or examples. Be sure your essay has a logical flow. There should be a reason for every sentence in your essay, such reasons include introducing a new example or detail to support the main idea, or explaining or supporting an example or detail mentioned previously. Do not write any sentences that are unrelated to your main idea or that do not fit into the organizational structure of your essay just to increase your word count.

- Make every effort to use effective language and appropriate sentence structure and vocabulary. Try NOT to use vocabulary or constructions that you are not confident with, as these will increase your chances of making errors.

- Use a variety of language. English has a large number of synonyms and analogous constructions, so using the same construction repeatedly is considered poor style.

- Keep the 50-minute time limit for the entire writing section in mind. Remember that raters are expecting to read drafted essays, not finely polished final products. If you find yourself stuck in a particular part of your essay, it is best to move on and complete the essay, then go back and fix the difficult area.

- Try to leave at least five minutes for revision. When revising, be sure to look for spelling or grammatical errors (remember, there is no spell checker on the test!) as well as ways to improve the structure and flow of your essay.

- You must answer each question as it appears. You can NOT return to any questions later.

- Do not leave any question unanswered. You are NOT penalized for guessing an answer.

Introduction to the *Basic Skills for the TOEFL® iBT* series

Basic Skills for the TOEFL® iBT is a 3-level, 12-book test preparation series designed for beginning-level students of the TOEFL® iBT. Over the course of the series, students build on their current vocabulary to include common TOEFL® and academic vocabulary. They are also introduced to the innovative questions types found on the TOEFL® iBT, and are provided with practice of TOEFL® iBT reading, listening, speaking, and writing passages, conversations, lectures, and questions accessible to students of their level.

Basic Skills for the TOEFL® iBT enables students to build on both their language skills and their knowledge. The themes of the passages, lectures, and questions cover topics often seen on the TOEFL® iBT. In addition, the independent topics, while taking place in a university setting, are also accessible to and understood by students preparing to enter university. The academic topics are also ones that native speakers study.

Students accumulate vocabulary over the series. Vocabulary learned at the beginning of the series will appear in passages and lectures later in the book, level, and series. Each level gets progressively harder. The vocabulary becomes more difficult, the number of vocabulary words to be learned increases, and the passages, conversations, and lectures get longer and increase in level. By the end of the series, students will know all 570 words on the standard Academic Word List (AWL) used by TESOL and have a solid foundation in and understanding of the TOEFL® iBT.

Not only will Basic Skills for the TOEFL® iBT start preparing students for the TOEFL® iBT, but it will also give students a well-rounded basis for either further academic study in English or further TOEFL® iBT study.

Introduction to the *Basic Skills for the TOEFL® iBT* Writing Book

This is the first writing book in the Basic Skills for the TOEFL® iBT series. In the independent section, the student will read two independent sample responses and then have an opportunity to write their own response. In the integrated section, they will read a passage, listen to a lecture, and fill in the blanks of a sample response. The student will then have an opportunity to give their own response based on a different reading passage and lecture. The lectures will be on the topics that the student was first introduced to in the first reading book and that have been developed over the listening and speaking books.

Each unit is separated into eight sections:

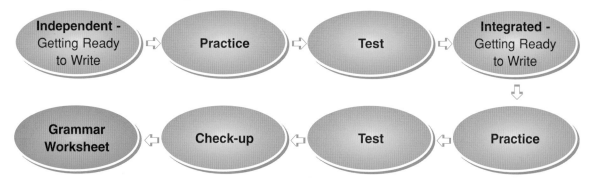

The following will outline the activities and aims of each section.

Independent - Getting Ready to Write

Key Vocabulary and TOEFL® Vocabulary

Students begin by studying the vocabulary they will encounter in the following section.
TOEFL® Vocabulary includes the words that have been found to appear most often in TOEFL®
preparation materials or are on the Academic Word List (AWL). TOEFL® Vocabulary includes the
most important words for the student to learn in order to build his or her vocabulary before further
TOEFL® study. **Key Vocabulary** includes the other words that are important for the student to
know in order to understand the essays that will follow.

Prompt

In this part, students are asked some simple questions about an experience in their own lives.
This introduces students to the theme of the independent section and gets students writing
about things that are familiar to them.

Practice

TOEFL® Question

Students read the question and prompt. This prompt will be used throughout the independent
section.

Sample Response 1

Students read a sample response and answer whether the writer agreed or disagreed with the
prompt. This lets students see one way of answering the question and introduces them to the
idea that any answer, so long as it is backed-up with reason, is acceptable.

Outline

Students now fill out an outline for the response. By reading the response, they will see what
information should be inserted into the outline. This will help student learn and become comfortable
with using outlines. It will also help them see how opinions, reasons, and examples are used within an
essay. Being able to write an outline during the TOEFL® test will enable students to structure their
essay well.

Students are then asked to underline transitional words or phrases in the response. This helps
students see how to connect their opinions, reasons, and examples.

Sample Response 2

Students read a second sample response and answer whether the writer agreed or disagreed with
the prompt. This response will take the opposite view from the first response. This lets students see
another way of answering the question.

The two sample responses use all the vocabulary words studied at the beginning of the independent
section.

Outline

Students now fill out an outline for the second response. By reading the response, they will see what information should be inserted into the outline. Again, this helps students become familiar with outlines.

Students are then asked to underline transitional words or phrases in the response. This helps students see how to connect their opinions, reasons, and examples.

TOEFL® Vocabulary Practice

Here, students find sentences that use the TOEFL® vocabulary that they learned at the beginning of the section. This helps students practice the words in context.

Test

The test contains the same prompt that the students read sample responses for. They will now have the opportunity to create their own response.

The test is split into four steps. The **first step** allows students to read the prompt as would happen in the actual TOEFL® test. The **second step** then enables them to decide whether they agree or disagree. The **third step** gives students outlines to fill in. The students will be expected to give two reasons for their opinions and two examples for each reason. The outline gives them a guided introduction and conclusion sentence. The **fourth step** allows the students to finally write an essay using their outlines. The spaces for their essays have transitional words or phrases to help the students connect their ideas.

The answer key gives two further responses that use many of the vocabulary words learned at the beginning of the section.

Integrated - Getting Ready to Write

Key Vocabulary and TOEFL® Vocabulary

Students begin by studying the vocabulary they will encounter in the following section. See the independent description for further details.

Reading Passage

Students will read the first part of a passage. They are then asked a question about the main idea and one question about what they think the rest of the reading passage and the lecture will be about. The aim is to introduce the students to the theme of the integrated section.

Lecture

Students will listen to the first part of a lecture that is related to the passage they read on the previous page. They are then asked a question about the lecture's main idea.

Note-taking

Students now read the full passage and listen to the full lecture while filling in notes. The notes are guided so that the students can fill in the parts that are missing. The reading passage and the lecture use all the vocabulary words studied at the beginning of the integrated section. The notes are written in a form that helps the students recognize the main idea, key points, and supporting details. This will enable the students to see how these can be used in the response.

Prompt

Students read the prompt. This will tell the students if the aim is to show how the reading supports the lecture or if it should show how the lecture refutes the passage.

Sample Response

Students see a sample response with four phrases removed. The students should use their notes to insert these phrases into the correct spaces. This sample response helps the students see how an integrated response may be structured.

TOEFL® Vocabulary Practice

Here, students find sentences that use the TOEFL® vocabulary that they learned at the beginning of the section. This helps the students practice the words in context.

The test is split into four steps. In **step one**, students take notes on the reading passage and lecture. In **step two**, they read and listen to the prompt. In **step three**, they complete an outline for their response. In **step four**, they write out a full essay.

The notes, outline, and essay are all guided to help the students recognize the main ideas, key points, supporting details, organization, and transitional phrases that would they would be expected to use in a well-written essay.

The Answer Key gives completed outlines and responses. In addition, the readings and lectures within the test use many of the vocabulary words learned at the beginning of the section.

Key Vocabulary Practice

Students review the key vocabulary learned over the course of the unit.
This helps the students practice these words in context.

Grammar Worksheet

At the end of the book, there is a grammar worksheet to go with each unit. The grammar worksheets are optional. They may be used in class, as homework, or not at all. The worksheets cover the following grammatical points:

Unit 1	Simple Sentences	Unit 2	Subject-Verb Agreement
Unit 3	Conjunctive Adverbs	Unit 4	Modals (*Should* & *Must*)
Unit 5	Confusing Verbs and Nouns	Unit 6	Simple Present and Verbs for Citing
Unit 7	*Will* for Prediction	Unit 8	Verb + Noun phrases (*Have, Make,* & *Take*)
Unit 9	Compound Sentences	Unit 10	Transitions for Presenting Supporting Points
Unit 11	Simple Present, Simple Past, and *Used to*	Unit 12	Transitions for Time and Sequence

Each worksheet is designed to go with its corresponding unit. The worksheet will use examples from the main unit in its activities, thereby connecting it to the main unit.

Introduction to the Writing Process

In this book, students are primarily shown the best ways to prepare for the writing section of the TOEFL® test. However, this is only part of the process. It is recommended that you also introduce students to the full process for writing. If students have an understanding of the whole process, they will find the TOEFL® test easier. Also, if students are familiar with the full process, they will be able to successfully write essays in English either at school, or university.

Organization is of extreme importance in ANY essay. The TOEFL® writing section is no different. By using the writing process below, students will learn how to write an organized essay.

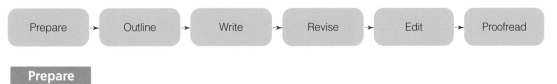

Prepare → Outline → Write → Revise → Edit → Proofread

Prepare

It is essential that you prepare for any essay. This includes a number of steps such as researching, deciding on an aim, brainstorming, and clustering.

Research
Researching for an essay entails finding reliable sources and taking notes from them. In the integrated section, you are given the sources you are to use—the reading passage and the lecture. In the independent section, you cannot do further research, so you should rely on your own knowledge and experiences.

Aim

You should then decide on the aim or thesis statement for your essay. In the TOEFL® iBT, you are given a prompt/question to answer, which is the aim.

Brainstorm and Cluster

Brainstorming involves writing down all of the ideas and thoughts you have on your subject. It is not meant to be well-organized, that will happen when you put these ideas into a cluster. Brainstorming is particularly useful for the independent section. The cluster is where you start to organize your ideas. Include only the items the brainstorming and your notes that actually fulfill the aim of your essay. Your main topic should go in a circle in the center with the main ideas and supporting details branching off it.

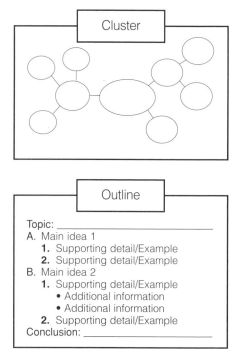

Outline

This is where you decide on the organization of the points from your cluster. You should ensure that they follow a logical order. You should also decide on your introductory (topic) sentence and your conclusion sentence. Remember that everything goes in groups. You can't have an A without a B or a 1 without a 2.

Outline

Topic: _____
A. Main idea 1
   1. Supporting detail/Example
   2. Supporting detail/Example
B. Main idea 2
   1. Supporting detail/Example
      • Additional information
      • Additional information
   2. Supporting detail/Example
Conclusion: _____

Write

You then follow the outline and write the first full draft of the essay. Do not worry too much about grammar, sentence structure, spelling, etc. as this will be addressed in the next stage.

Revise

Read your essay and ensure that the flow of the essay is what you were aiming for and that the essay addresses the set question. Make any necessary changes.

Edit

Check the flow again, and also edit for grammar, spelling, etc.

Proofread

Read the essay one last time and focus on any final punctuation, grammar, and spelling errors.

It should be made clear to students that the people who grade the TOEFL® essays expect to see first drafts. This should also be kept in mind when marking the essays submitted for this course. Students should, however; polish their essays as much as they can during the TOEFL® test, and they should make sure to proofread their work at least once.

Basic Skills for the TOEFL® iBT

Sample Writing Lesson Plan - 50 minutes

Homework Check	5 min.	• Check that students completed their homework, and talk about any problems they had.
Review	5 min.	• Review the strategies discussed in the previous unit, and talk about other strategies students might have employed while doing their homework. • Compare the answers different students gave in their homework, and ask some students to read out their essay in front of the class. All students should have to do this at least once over the course of the book. • The class should proofread one another's essays and evaluate them using the form at the back of the book.

Main Lesson	35 min.	* This is a plan for teaching the integrated section in class. However, the independent and integrated sections may also be alternately taught in the classroom.
		
		Integrated - Getting Ready to Write
		A. Learn the words.
		  • Preview the vocabulary and have students read the words aloud.
		  • Talk about what parts of speech the words belong to.
		B. Read the prompt. Then answer the questions.
		  • Have the students read the passage and then answer the questions with a partner.
		  • As a class, predict what the rest of the passage and the lecture will be about.
		
		Practice
		A. Lecture
		  • Have the students listen to the lecture and then answer the questions with a partner.
		B. Note-taking
		  • Have students take notes while they read and listen.
		  • Ask students to compare their notes with a classmate, and ensure they all have the main information. Emphasize that each student's notes may be written differently, but that all of the notes should include the same main points.
		C. Prompt
		  • Read the prompt as a class, and discuss the meaning of it. Make sure that everyone understands the prompt.
		  • With books closed, do a cluster, outline, and response to the prompt as a class.
		D. Sample Response
		  • Put students into groups, and tell them to read the sample response and fill in the blanks.
		  • In groups or as a class, compare the sample response with the class response while indicating the differences.
		  • If time allows, have each group write an outline for the sample response.
		E. TOEFL® Vocabulary Practice
		  • Ask students to complete the sentences and check their answers in pairs.
		
		Test
		  • Students should complete the test individually.
		  • Then compare outlines and responses with a partner. They should evaluate each other's essay using the form at the back of the book.
		
		Independent - Getting Ready to Write (Next unit)
		Talk about the topics of the Independent section. Quickly brainstorm during which students can pick up ideas and useful expressions from their teacher and classmates as well as the book.

Wrap-up	5 min.	• Give homework (the rest of the independent section.) • The students should have to show that they completed the full writing process for the Independent Test. Their brainstorming, clustering, and the edited final of their essay should be in their notebooks. * The Integrated Test, the check-up, or the worksheet can also be given as homework.

Teaching Tips

- It is strongly recommended that the class go through the target vocabulary prior to starting the rest of the unit.

- It is a good idea to have students make their own vocabulary lists on their PCs or in notebooks. Putting the words under thematic categories (categories of subjects) would be an effective way to study the words.

- It is important to emphasize the understanding of the main idea of the lectures. Students often listen without constructing the framework, which could cause them problems in understanding the main points and how they relate to the passage and the prompt.

- During the first class, take time to introduce the writing process and, in particular, the outline format. Then, when students are asked to use the outlines later, they will be familiar with the format and not as intimidated.

- In the beginning, the note-taking practice needs to be done in class with the teacher's assistance because not many students are familiar with note-taking. Gradually, have students take notes in groups, pairs, and then individually.

- Timing students is an effective activity. Teachers can give a target length of time to complete the essay and decrease it over the course of the book or series. Encourage students to do timed-activities even when they do their homework.

- Students should read one another's essays and evaluate them.

- Students can use the definitions and synonyms in the vocabulary section when they write their essays.

- Use the test at the end of each section, to check students' progress. Their essays should improve in organization, quality, and length as they study.

[01] Independent

Getting Ready to Write

A. Learn the words.

Key Vocabulary

offer	to put something forward for others to take or refuse
as a result	therefore
future	the time still to come

TOEFL® Vocabulary

severe	serious; extreme
competition	a contest to perform better than others at something
faith	the belief in something by someone
guidance	helpful advice
firm	strong

B. Read the prompt. Then answer the questions.

> Describe an experience you recently shared with your family.

1. What was the experience?

I _____ with my family.

2. Why did you do this?

We did this because _____.

3. Did your family enjoy this experience?

My family _____.

4. Do you think this experience was important to your family?

I think that _____.

Practice

A. Read the question.

Do you agree or disagree with the following statement?

Family is less important now than it was in the past.

Use specific reasons and examples to support your answer.

Sample Response 1

B. Read the sample response. Then answer the question.

I think that family is just as important as it was in the past. There are two reasons why I feel this way. First, kids today need more support than ever before. Families offer lots of support. There is a lot of severe competition in the world today. Last year, I tried out for a youth Olympic soccer team. The other players were very talented. I did not think I was good enough. My family supported me. They had faith in me. I made the team. I don't think I would have without their support. Also, I think that families are more important now because family members can offer lots of guidance. I feel that kids make more bad choices today. Kids need loving families to guide them. Then they will make the right decisions for their futures. Therefore, I believe families are more important now.

Which side of the statement does the response take?
(A) Agree   (B) Disagree

Outline

C. Complete the outline for the response.

Topic: Family is _____ important now.
  A. Kids need more _____
      1. Tried out for youth Olympic _____
      2. Would not have made the team _____
  B. Families offer lots of _____
      1. Kids make more bad _____
      2. Kids need loving families to _____
Conclusion: I believe families are _____.

D. Underline the transitional words or phrases in the sample response.

E. Read the sample response. Then answer the question.

    I think that family is less important now than in the past for two reasons. To begin with, family members do not seem to care about being together much anymore. I think, in the past, it was more important for families to spend time together. For example, my grandparents had a firm rule about eating dinner together as a family every night. Today, my mom and dad are very busy. They are not even home at the same time. Also, family members do not help each other like they used to. A long time ago, families had to stay together to take care of each other. Today, many families don't live near each other. My mom and her brother live far from each other. As a result, they have not even seen each other in six years. For these reasons, I think family is less important now.

Which side of the statement does the response take?

(A) Agree   (B) Disagree

Outline

F. Complete the outline for the response.

Topic: Family is _____ important now.
A. Family members do not seem to care about _____
    1. Grandparents had a firm rule about _____
    2. Today mom and dad aren't home _____
B. Families members do not _____
    1. Families used to stay together to _____
    2. Mom and her brother _____
Conclusion: For these reasons, I think family _____.

G. Underline the transitional words or phrases in the sample response.

TOEFL® Vocabulary Practice

H. Fill in the blanks with the correct words.

faith	firm	guidance	competition	severe

1. The job of a school counselor is to offer students _____.
2. _____ sometimes requires believing in something that cannot be seen.
3. There is often fierce _____ among students in the best medical schools.
4. _____ weather causes millions of dollars of damage every year.
5. Leaders need to be able to make _____ decisions and stand by them.

Test

Step 1

Read the question.

Do you agree or disagree with the following statement?

Family is less important now than it was in the past.

Use specific reasons and examples to support your answer.

Step 2

State your opinion.

I _____ with the statement.

Step 3

Write an outline for your essay that will support your opinion.

Topic: Family is _____ important now.

A. _____

    1. _____

    2. _____

B. _____

    1. _____

    2. _____

Conclusion: This is why I feel that family is _____.

Step 4

Complete the response using your outline from above.

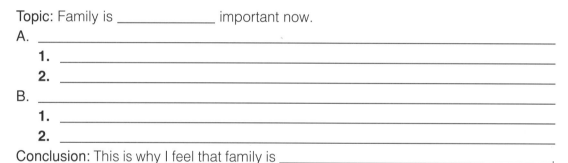

    I think that family is _____ important now than it was in the past.

I think this because _____.

For example, _____

_____.

I also believe this because _____.

For example, _____

_____.

This is why I feel that family is _____.

Integrated - History

Getting Ready to Write

A. Learn the words.

Key Vocabulary

vote	to express a personal choice in a formal way about issues or leaders
seemingly	appearing to have a quality that is not true
tax	an amount of money the government makes people pay

TOEFL® Vocabulary

adopt	to start to use an idea or belief
social	concerned with human society and welfare
legal	allowed according to the law
permit	to allow to do something
arrest	to take to jail

Reading Passage

B. Read the first part of a passage. Then answer the questions.

> ### Slavery
>
> Slavery began in the US in the 1600s. It was banned in 1865. African Americans were now free. However, they were not treated the same as others. New laws were adopted in the American South. These laws did not support equal rights. They had many effects on African Americans.

1. What is the main idea of the passage?

    (A) The effects of certain laws on African Americans

    (B) The comparison of political and social freedoms

2. What do you think the rest of the passage and the lecture will talk about? Write two or three ideas below.

    _____

    _____

Practice

A. **Listen to the first part of a lecture. Then answer the question.** `Track 1`

What is the main idea of the lecture?

(A) A description of laws that didn't support African American equal rights

(B) The effects of new equal rights laws

Note-taking

B. **Read the full passage. Then listen to the full lecture. Take notes in the boxes below.** `Track 2`

> ### Slavery
>
> Slavery began in the US in the 1600s. It was banned in 1865. African Americans were then free. However, they were not treated the same as others. New laws were adopted in the American South. These laws did not support equal rights. They had many effects on African Americans.
>
> First, they did not let African Americans have political freedom. New voting laws made people pay to vote. Many African Americans could not afford this seemingly small cost.
>
> Second, these laws did not give them real social freedom. It was not legal for African Americans to use the same areas as others. They had to use different train cars and restrooms. These unfair laws were called Jim Crow laws.

Reading

Main idea: The effects of two types _____

Key points:
- The laws did not support _____
- African Americans did not have _____
  - Many African Americans could not afford to _____
- The laws did not give African Americans _____
  - African Americans could not use _____

Lecture

Main idea: New laws _____

Key points:
- Poll taxes stopped many African Americans from _____
  - Fifty-percent-fewer _____
- Jim Crow laws made it OK to _____
  - The areas were supposed to be _____

C. Read the prompt.

Summarize the main points made in the lecture and explain how they support the main points in the reading passage.

Sample Response

D. Fill in the blanks of the sample response using phrases from the box. Use your notes to help you.

The reading explains how _____ in the American South did not support equal rights for African Americans. These laws _____ political or social freedoms. The lecture illustrates how this was true.

The speaker says that poll taxes kept African Americans from voting. The speaker says that in one state _____ African Americans voted because of these taxes.

The speaker also explains that Jim Crow laws unfairly separated African Americans from other people. The areas _____ separate but equal. However, they were not. African Americans could not use the same nice areas as others.

were supposed to be	laws adopted
fifty-percent-fewer	did not allow

TOEFL® Vocabulary Practice

E. Fill in the blanks with the correct words.

social	adopt	arrests	permit	legal

1. Birthday parties are just one type of _____ gathering.
2. Companies often _____ new policies to make business run better.
3. Airlines do not _____ people to carry large bags on board.
4. Different countries have different ideas about what is _____ and what is illegal.
5. Each time a police officer _____ someone, they have to file a report.

Test

Step 1

🎧 **Read the passage. Then listen to the lecture. Take notes in the boxes below.** `Track 3`

Jim Crow Laws

Jim Crow laws did not allow African Americans to be treated fairly. This treatment happened because the highest court in the US said it was OK. The Supreme Court made two decisions that permitted this unfair treatment.

First, the court took away the Civil Rights Act of 1875. This law was about fairness. It allowed all people to use the areas they wanted. The court said this law was no longer a law.

Second, the court made it legal to make African Americans use separate places. The court said that the places were separate but equal. So they said it was fair to make rules that separated people. These two decisions made it OK to make Jim Crow laws.

Reading

Main idea: The Supreme Court permitted African Americans to be treated unfairly.
Key points:
- Court took away the _____
  - This law had allowed all people to _____
- Court made it legal to allow separate but _____

Lecture

Main idea: How Jim Crow laws first started.
Key points:
- After Civil Rights Act of 1875 was gone, southern states _____
  - African Americans couldn't _____
- Homer Plessy went _____
  - They said it was OK for him _____

Step 2

🎧 **Read and listen to the prompt.** `Track 4`

Summarize the main points made in the lecture and explain how they support the main points in the reading passage.

Step 3

Complete the outline using your notes from Step 1.

Topic: The reading and the lecture are about the removal of the Civil Rights Act of 1875 and the start of _____.

A. The Supreme Court permitted _____

    1. They removed the _____

    2. They made it legal to allow separate _____

B. Southern states started adopting _____

    1. African Americans couldn't ride _____

    2. The court said it was OK for Homer Plessy to _____

Conclusion: The lecture supports the reading because it gives examples of how these laws allowed African Americans to be treated unfairly.

Step 4

Complete the response using your outline from Step 3.

    The reading and the lecture are about _____
_____.

The reading says that the Supreme Court permitted African Americans to be treated unfairly by _____.

    The lecture explains that after this, southern states started adopting lots of Jim Crow laws. For example, _____.

The lecture also talks about Homer Plessy who went to court. The court said _____
_____.

    The lecture supports the reading because _____
_____.

Check-up

Fill in the blanks with the correct words.

as a result	vote	offer	seemingly	future	tax

1. Many universities _____ scholarship programs that help many students.
2. In America, citizens are allowed to _____ when they turn eighteen.
3. In the _____, robots will be able to live with and assist people who need help at home.
4. Even _____ large planets like Jupiter are small when compared to the size of the sun.
5. Many people complain that the _____ laws the government creates are unfair.
6. Italy scored more goals than France in the soccer World Cup final. _____, they won.

[02] Independent

Getting Ready to Write

A. Learn the words.

Key Vocabulary

train	to teach someone how to do a job
lawyer	a person whose job is to give legal advice
secretary	a person whose job is to assist others with office duties

TOEFL® Vocabulary

relative	a family member
flaw	an imperfection; a weakness
hardly	barely; almost not at all
multiply	to add a number to itself many times
perfect	without any problems

B. Read the prompt. Then answer the questions.

Describe a time when someone had to teach you something.

1. Who was the person teaching you?
   It was _____.

2. What did he/she teach you?
   He/she taught me _____.

3. How did you feel about learning this?
   I felt _____.

4. What made him/her a good teacher?
   He/she was _____.

Practice

A. Read the question.

Do you agree or disagree with the following statement?

Parents make the best teachers.

Use specific reasons and examples to support your answer.

Sample Response 1

B. Read the sample response. Then answer the question.

I think that parents do make the best teachers. I feel this way for two reasons. First of all, they know you the best. A relative like a mom or dad spends the most time around you. They know the things you do well. They also know your flaws. A new teacher hardly knows you at all. It might take a teacher a long time to notice that you can multiply big numbers easily, but that you find geometry hard to do. The second reason is that parents know how to keep their kids interested. My dad knows how to keep me interested in my homework longer. For example, he lets me build my math problems. I like doing my math when I can make models of the problems. I feel that parents are great teachers. They know you best and know how to keep you interested in learning.

Which side of the statement does the response take?
(A) Agree   (B) Disagree

Outline

C. Complete the outline for the response.

Topic: Parents _____ make the best teachers.
A. Parents know you _____
   1. They know
     • the things you do _____
     • your _____
   2. Takes a teacher a long time to notice that
     • you can _____
     • you find geometry _____
B. Parents know how to keep kids _____
   1. Dad lets me _____
   2. I like to make models of _____
Conclusion: I feel that parents are _____.

D. Underline the transitional words or phrases in the sample response.

E. Read the sample response. Then answer the question.

I can say for sure that parents do not make the best teachers. First of all, teachers have been trained to teach you. They went to college to learn how to teach in the best way. Parents usually have other jobs such as lawyers, secretaries, or firefighters. This means they know how to do other things. My dad is a farmer. He drives a tractor all day. He knows a lot about science and machinery. However, even he says he doesn't know much about geometry. Secondly, regular teachers treat all the students the same. Parents wouldn't be fair. For example, my mom expects a lot from me. If she taught my class, I would have to know all the answers. I would have to be perfect too! Parents should not be teachers. They have no training and might not be fair.

Which side of the statement does the response take?

(A) Agree   (B) Disagree

Outline

F. Complete the outline for the response.

Topic: Parents _____ make the best teachers.

A. Teachers have been _____ to teach, parents haven't.
  1. Teachers went to _____
  2. Parents have other _____
  3. My father knows a lot about science, but not _____
B. Teachers treat students the same.
  1. Parents wouldn't be _____
  2. Mom would expect me to be _____
Conclusion: Parents _____ be teachers.

G. Underline the transitional words or phrases in the sample response.

TOEFL® Vocabulary Practice

H. Fill in the blanks with the correct words.

flaw	hardly	multiply	perfect	relatives

1. A _____ exam score is often very hard to get.

2. It is not wise to make an important agreement with someone you _____ know.

3. Family reunions are a great way to get to know distant _____.

4. Children must learn how to _____ before they learn how to divide.

5. The best diamonds are the ones without a single _____.

Test

Step 1

Read the question.

Do you agree or disagree with the following statement?

Parents make the best teachers.

Use specific reasons and examples to support your answer.

Step 2

State your opinion.

I _____ with the statement.

Step 3

Write an outline for your essay that will support your decision.

Topic: Parents _____ make the best teachers.

A. _____

    1. _____

    2. _____

B. _____

    1. _____

    2. _____

Conclusion: I think that _____.

Step 4

Complete the response using your outline from above.

    I think that parents _____ make the best teachers.

This is because _____.

An example is _____

_____.

In my experience, _____

_____.

For these reasons, I think that _____.

Integrated - Art

Getting Ready to Write

A. Learn the words.

Key Vocabulary

cubism	a geometric style of painting and sculpture
fan	a person who admires someone else or their work
unusual	different

TOEFL® Vocabulary

tragic	very sad
humanity	human nature
era	a period of time
imitate	to copy or be like something
appreciate	to understand the good qualities in someone or something

Reading Passage

B. Read the first part of a passage. Then answer the questions.

Pablo Picasso

Pablo Picasso was a famous modern artist. He was born in 1881. He is best known for his style of art. This style is called cubism. Many people did not like Picasso's painting for two reasons.

The first reason is that his paintings seemed tragic.

1. What is the main idea of the passage?

(A) Types of modern art

(B) Why people did not like Picasso's art

2. What do you think the rest of the passage and the lecture will talk about? Write two or three ideas below.

_____

_____

Practice

Lecture

A. Listen to the first part of a lecture. Then answer the question. `Track 5`

What is the main idea of the lecture?

(A) Discussing people who liked Picasso's art

(B) Discussing people who did not like Picasso's art

Note-taking

B. Read the full passage. Then listen to the full lecture. Take notes in the boxes below. `Track 6`

> ### Pablo Picasso
>
> Pablo Picasso was a famous modern artist. He was born in 1881. He is best known for his style of art. This style is called cubism. Many people did not like Picasso's painting for two reasons.
>
> The first reason is that his paintings seemed tragic. The people in his paintings looked poor. They seemed sad, too. This showed a different side of humanity. People in that era wanted art to make them feel good.
>
> The second reason is that his art did not look real. His work imitated things he saw in daily life. However, he found a different beauty in common things. He used squares and triangles for people's shapes. It tested people's ideas of art.

Reading

Main idea: Reasons why people did not _____

Key points:
- Picasso's art seemed _____
  - People looked _____
- Picasso's art did not _____
  - He used _____

Lecture

Main idea: There were many people who _____

Key points:
- Picasso had many _____
- Many people liked the _____
  - *Boy with a Pipe* sold for _____
- Many critics also _____
  - Apollinaire was the most important _____
  - He was one of the first to notice _____

C. Read the prompt.

Summarize the main points made in the lecture and explain how they challenge the main points in the reading passage.

Sample Response

D. Fill in the blanks of the sample response using phrases from the box. Use your notes to help you.

The reading explains why people did not like Picasso's tragic art. They did not like how he made people look sad and poor. They also did not like his

_____.

The lecture shows that many people really did think that Picasso was a great artist. The speaker says that many _____ Picasso's work. The speaker says one painting sold for 104 million dollars.

The speaker also says that _____ liked Picasso's art as well. A very important critic, Apollinaire, noticed Picasso's _____ first. The lecture shows that many people did like Picasso.

great talent	fans appreciated
style of cubism	many art critics

TOEFL® Vocabulary Practice

E. Fill in the blanks with the correct words.

appreciate	era	humanity	imitate	tragic

1. During the jazz _____, night clubs became popular.
2. Younger siblings often _____ what their older siblings do.
3. Musicians like to write songs about _____.
4. Movies about war usually have _____ scenes.
5. A good teacher will _____ a student's hard work.

Test

Step 1

🔊 Read the passage. Then listen to the lecture. Take notes in the boxes below. `Track 7`

Picasso's Blue Period

Picasso's life and unusual art can be split into different periods. One is named the blue period. This came before his cubism period. He painted scenes about humanity. He used mostly blue colors. There were two reasons why.

To begin with, he was not happy with the politics of the era. He felt that poor people were not treated well. He felt sorry for them.

Next, Picasso was an unhappy artist. He painted a self-portrait at this time. He was only twenty years old. However, he looks pale, sad, and much older in it. His art often imitated his own life.

Reading

Main idea: Picasso's _____
Key points:
- Picasso did not like _____
- Picasso felt that poor people _____
- Picasso's self-portrait shows that he was _____
  - In his self-portrait, he looks _____

Lecture

Main idea: The real causes for Picasso's _____
Key points:
- One of Picasso's close friends _____
- Picasso no longer _____
- Picasso was alone and _____
  - He lived away from home _____

Step 2

🔊 Read and listen to the prompt. `Track 8`

Summarize the main points made in the lecture and explain how they challenge the main points in the reading passage.

Step 3

Complete the outline using your notes from Step 1.

Topic: The reading and the lecture are about Picasso's _____.
A. The reading says his blue period started because
    1. he did not like _____
    2. he thought poor people were _____
    3. he was an unhappy artist as shown in his _____
B. The lecture says his blue period started because
    1. his good _____
    2. he was poor and living away from _____
Conclusion: The lecture challenges the reading by offering different causes for
            Picasso's blue period.

Step 4

Complete the response using your outline from Step 3.

    The reading and the lecture are about _____.
The reading says that the blue period happened because Picasso did not like
_____. It says he thought _____.
The reading also says Picasso was an _____ because he looked
very unhappy in _____.
    However, the lecture gives another reason for how _____.
The speaker challenges the reading by saying that Picasso's good friend _____
_____.
    The lecture challenges the reading by _____
_____.

Check-up

Fill in the blanks with the correct words.

| fans | train | lawyer | unusual | secretary | cubism |

1. _____ uses shapes to make art.

2. Snakes have _____ patterns on their skin.

3. Automotive schools _____ people to become mechanics.

4. There are usually thousands of _____ at a baseball game.

5. Big companies usually hire a _____ to make sure all their business activities are legal.

6. A _____ usually answers the phone in a big company.

[03] Independent

Getting Ready to Write

A. Learn the words.

Key Vocabulary

appearance	the way someone looks
trendy	in style
magazine	a paper book of photographs and articles produced usually once a month

TOEFL® Vocabulary

reflect	to show
worth	value
conscious	aware of
beauty	the quality of being pleasant to look at
brand	a name given to products by the companies that make them

B. Read the prompt. Then answer the questions.

> Describe something you do to help your appearance.

1. What is it that you do?

The thing I do is _____.

2. Why do you do this?

I do this because _____.

3. Why is your appearance important to you?

I think that it _____.

4. Do you think you care too much about doing this?

I think that _____. Therefore, I should _____

_____.

Practice

A. Read the question.

Do you agree or disagree with the following statement?

People care too much about their appearance and being fashionable.

Use specific reasons and examples to support your answer.

Sample Response 1

B. Read the sample response. Then answer the question.

I think people do care too much about appearance and fashion. Some people have to buy the most popular clothes. These people think clothes reflect who they are. My friend Tom spends his money on trendy clothes. I don't think clothes are worth it. Also, I think people are too self-conscious. My friend Tracy wears high heel shoes most of the time. They hurt her feet. However, she thinks they look good, so she wears them. Another friend reads too many beauty magazines. Therefore, I think people are happier when they do not worry so much about fashion and appearance.

Which side of the statement does the response take?
(A) Agree   (B) Disagree

Outline

C. Complete the outline for the response.

Topic: People _____ about appearance and fashion.
A. People buy _____
    1. People think clothes _____
    2. My friend spends money on _____
B. People are too self- _____
    1. My friend wears _____
       • They hurt _____
       • She thinks _____
    2. My friend reads too many _____
Conclusion: I think people are happier when _____.

D. Underline the transitional words or phrases in the sample response.

E. Read the sample response. Then answer the question.

I think people do not care too much about appearance and fashion. First, I think it is good to care about beauty. People should want to look good. I care about how I look, but I do not worry about it. Also, I do not think people care too much about being fashionable. People like to wear nice clothes. Some clothes are popular because they are made well, not just because of a brand name. I wear a lot of the popular brands because they make clothes that I like. I am conscious of how I look. However, I do not think about it all the time. I think most people are this way.

Which side of the statement does the response take?

(A) Agree   (B) Disagree

Outline

F. Complete the outline for the response.

Topic: People _____ about appearance and fashion.
A. It is good to _____
    1. People should want to look _____
    2. I care about _____
B. People like to wear nice _____
    1. Some clothes are _____
    2. I wear popular _____
Conclusion: I am conscious of how I look, but _____.

G. Underline the transitional words or phrases in the sample response.

TOEFL® Vocabulary Practice

H. Fill in the blanks with the correct words.

reflect	worth	conscious	beauty	brand

1. An airplane is _____ more money than a car.

2. The surface of calm water will _____ an image.

3. Coca cola is one popular _____ name known throughout the world.

4. _____ is just one thing that makes a person attractive.

5. Kind people are always _____ of how they make others feel.

Test

Step 1

Read the question.

Do you agree or disagree with the following statement?

People care too much about their appearance and being fashionable.

Use specific reasons and examples to support your answer.

Step 2

State your opinion.

I _____ with the statement.

Step 3

Write an outline for your essay that will support your opinion.

Topic: I _____ people care too much about appearances.
A. _____
    1. _____
    2. _____
B. _____
    1. _____
    2. _____
Conclusion: This is why I _____ about appearances and fashion.

Step 4

Complete the response using your outline from above.

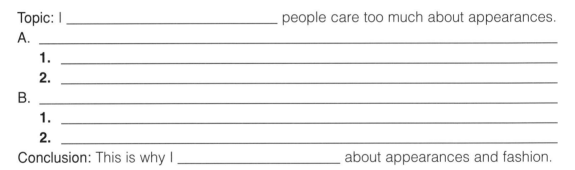

    I _____ people care too much about appearances.
First, I think _____.
For example, _____
_____.
Second, _____.
For example, _____
_____.
This is why I _____ about appearances and fashion.

Integrated - Zoology

Getting Ready to Write

A. Learn the words.

outward	on the outside
digestive	relating to how food is used by the body
tract	a group of related parts of the body

TOEFL® Vocabulary

trait	a feature or quality about something
strike	to attack; to hit
instinct	an inborn feeling to do something
storage	space for holding something
diet	the food usually eaten by a living thing

Reading Passage

B. Read the first part of a passage. Then answer the questions.

> **Carnivores**
>
> Carnivores are animals that mainly eat meat. They have traits on the outside and the inside that are made for eating meat.
>
> First, their outward traits help them catch and chew other animals. They have sharp claws to strike their prey. They also have sharp teeth to chew through tough skin and bones.

1. What is the main idea of the passage?

   (A) Types of animals that are carnivores

   (B) The traits of a carnivore

2. What do you think the rest of the passage and the lecture will talk about? Write two or three ideas below.

   _____

   _____

Practice

Lecture

A. Listen to the first part of a lecture. Then answer the question. `Track 9`

What is the main idea of the lecture?

(A) Identifying carnivore traits in tigers

(B) Comparing the behaviors of large cats

Note-taking

B. Read the full passage. Then listen to the full lecture. Take notes in the boxes below. `Track 10`

> ### Carnivores
>
> Carnivores are animals that mainly eat meat. They have traits on the outside and the inside that are made for eating meat.
>
> First, their outward traits help them catch and chew other animals. They have sharp claws to strike their prey. They also have sharp teeth to chew through tough skin and bones.
>
> They also have inside traits made for meat eating. They have simple stomachs. They do not have the instinct to eat plants all day long like some animals. So, they do not need more than one stomach for food storage. Their whole digestive tract is shorter because of their diet. This helps them break down the meat more quickly.

Reading

Main idea: Carnivores are built for _____

Key points:
- A carnivore's outward traits _____
  - They have _____
- A carnivore's inside traits are made for _____
  - They have _____
  - Their digestive tracts are _____

Lecture

Main idea: The carnivore traits of _____

Key points:
- A tiger's claws _____
  - A tiger's teeth are ten times _____
- A tiger's stomach _____
- A tiger's digestive tract is _____
  - A plant-eating animal's is _____

C. Read the prompt.

Summarize the main points made in the lecture and explain how they support the main points in the reading passage.

Sample Response

D. Fill in the blanks of the sample response using phrases from the box. Use your notes to help you.

The reading describes the outward and inside traits of a carnivore. These traits help a carnivore _____. The lecture uses a tiger as an example to describe the traits of a carnivore. The speaker says that a tiger has _____ that it uses to catch and eat its prey. The speaker says a tiger's claws are five inches long. The speaker also describes the tiger's simple stomach and short _____. Its digestive tract is only five times the _____. A plant-eating animal has a much longer digestive tract.

catch and eat animals	sharp teeth and claws
digestive tract	length of its body

TOEFL® Vocabulary Practice

E. Fill in the blanks with the correct words.

trait	strike	instinct	storage	diet

1. A healthy _____ includes fruit and vegetables.
2. A good sense of humor is just one desirable _____ people look for in others.
3. Cows have four stomachs for food _____.
4. An animal's _____ tells it when it is hungry and needs to find food.
5. A snake will _____ very quickly when it is threatened.

Test

Step 1

🎧 **Read the passage. Then listen to the lecture. Take notes in the boxes below.** `Track 11`

> ### Changing Animals
>
> Animals change over time. Some animals started out eating meat. Over time their diet changed. It changed from meat to plants. This was probably because there was not much prey left in the areas they lived.
>
> These animals started using their carnivore traits to eat plants. Their strong jaws helped them crush thick plants. Their sharp teeth helped them take the hard coverings off thick plants. However, they had a hard time digesting plants. Therefore, they only digested a little of what they ate.

Reading

Main idea: Animals can change from eating _____
Key points:
  • Diet changed because there was _____
  • Animals use their _____
    - They have a hard time _____

Lecture

Main idea: Pandas are carnivores that _____
Key points:
  • Pandas eat bamboo using their strong _____
  • A panda doesn't _____
    - It only digests _____
    - It eats for sixteen _____

Step 2

🎧 **Read and listen to the prompt.** `Track 12`

Summarize the main points made in the lecture and explain how they support the main points in the reading passage.

Step 3

Complete the outline using your notes from Step 1.

Topic: The reading and the lecture are about how an animal can change from being a plant eater to a meat eater.

A. The reading says
  1. that the animals changed because their _____
  2. they started using their _____
B. The lecture says
  1. this is true for the _____
  2. the panda uses its _____
C. The reading says that these animals have a hard time _____
D. The lecture says the panda does not digest _____
  1. It digests twenty percent _____
  2. It eats for sixteen _____
Conclusion: The lecture supports the points made in the reading by using the panda as an example.

Step 4

Complete the response using your outline from Step 3.

> The reading and the lecture are about _____
> _____.
> The reading says that the animals changed because _____.
> Therefore, they started _____ to eat tough plants.
> The lecture discusses how this is true _____. The speaker
> says that the panda _____ to eat plants.
> The reading says that these animals _____.
> The speaker also supports this by talking about how the panda _____
> _____.
>
> It only digests _____.
> The lecture supports the _____
> _____.

Check-up

Fill in the blanks with the correct words.

digestive	appearance	tract	outward	trendy	magazines

1. People often remodel their homes to improve its _____.

2. There are lots of types of _____, such as ones about cars, music, and fashion.

3. Teenagers usually feel the most comfortable wearing _____ clothing styles.

4. Eating fiber promotes good _____ health.

5. When we eat, food goes through the digestive _____.

6. Many people think _____ beauty is less important than personality.

[04] Independent

Getting Ready to Write

A. Learn the words.

Key Vocabulary

motion	movement
mumble	to speak in a low unclear voice
aloud	in a voice loud enough to be heard

TOEFL® Vocabulary

impression	a feeling you get from an experience
response	an answer or reply
interview	a formal meeting where questions are asked and answered
nervous	feeling worried, afraid, or excited
convey	to share an idea

B. Read the prompt. Then answer the questions.

> Describe an experience when you had to speak in front of people.

1. What was the experience?
It was _____.

2. Why did you do this?
Because _____.

3. How did you feel about this experience?
I felt that _____.

4. Do you think this experience was good for you?
I think that _____.

Practice

A. Read the question.

Do you agree or disagree with the following statement?

It is better to write well than to speak well.

Use specific reasons and examples to support your answer.

Sample Response 1

B. Read the sample response. Then answer the question.

I think that being able to write well is not as important as being able to speak well. I believe this is true for two reasons. The first reason is that giving a good first impression to someone is important. This can be based on what you say. For example, when you have an interview for a job, you will be asked questions. You have to speak clearly. Your responses cannot be one word sentences. The second reason is that you must be able to speak well on the phone. In our culture, most people have a cell phone. Most people do not want to hear a nervous person mumbling on the phone. You need to be able to convey what you want aloud. Therefore, I believe speaking well is more important than writing well.

Which side of the statement does the response take?
(A) Agree   (B) Disagree

Outline

C. Complete the outline for the response.

Topic: Writing well _____ speaking well.
A. First impressions are based on _____
    1. When you interview for a job, you have to speak _____
    2. When you interview for a job, your responses can't be _____
B. Must be able to speak well on the _____
    1. People don't want to hear _____
    2. You need to _____
Conclusion: I believe _____.

D. Underline the transitional words or phrases in the sample response.

E. Read the sample response. Then answer the question.

I feel that it is better to write well than to speak well. I think this way for two reasons. First of all, to get a job, you have to write well. You might have to write a letter about work experience. If you write poorly, you give a poor impression of yourself. You may not even get the chance to go for an interview. Secondly, our culture uses email to get things done. People send written messages all the time. You have to convey your opinions clearly. For example, they can't hear your voice or see hand motions in an email. You have to write well to be understood. These are the reasons why I think it is more important to write well than to speak well.

Which side of the statement does the response take?

(A) Agree   (B) Disagree

Outline

F. Complete the outline for the response.

Topic: It is better to _____.
A. To get a job you have to _____
   1. You might have to write a _____
   2. Writing poorly gives a _____
B. Our culture uses _____
   1. You have to send _____
   2. You have to convey _____
Conclusion: I believe it is more important _____.

G. Underline the transitional words or phrases in the sample response.

TOEFL® Vocabulary Practice

H. Fill in the blanks with the correct words.

convey	interview	impression	nervous	response

1. The _____ you make is important when you meet someone for the first time.
2. It's best to give a clear, confident _____ when asked a question during an interview.
3. Employees can become confused if the boss does not _____ clear instructions.
4. Employers like to _____ someone before giving them a job.
5. Many students find it is hard not to be _____ on the first day of school.

Test

Step 1

Read the question.

Do you agree or disagree with the following statement?

It is more important to speak well than to write well.

Use specific reasons and examples to support your answer.

Step 2

State your opinion.

I _____ with the statement.

Step 3

Write an outline for your essay that will support your opinion.

Topic: I think it is better to _____.
A. _____
    1. _____
    2. _____
B. _____
    1. _____
    2. _____
Conclusion: I think it is better to _____.

Step 4

Complete the response using your outline from above.

I think it is better to _____.
This is because _____.
For example, _____
_____.
Another reason is _____.
An example is _____
_____.
For these reasons, I think it is better to _____.

Integrated - Physics

Getting Ready to Write

A. Learn the words.

Key Vocabulary

prism	an object that breaks up a beam of light
pattern	a design of lines, shapes, or colors that repeat in a regular way
spectrum	the band of colors in a rainbow

TOEFL® Vocabulary

experiment	to test or try an idea
wave	a vibration going through the air
plain	simple or ordinary
compose	to form or make up
scatter	to spread out

Reading Passage

B. Read the first part of a passage. Then answer the questions.

> **Prisms**
>
> Have you ever experimented with a prism? It is a great way to understand more about colors and light.
>
> The first thing a prism does is refract light. This means that it changes the direction of the light as it passes through the prism.

1. What is the main idea of the passage?

   (A) A prism's effect on colors and light

   (B) The colors of a prism

2. What do you think the rest of the passage and the lecture will talk about? Write two or three ideas below.

   _____

   _____

Practice

Lecture

A. Listen to the first part of a lecture. Then answer the question. `Track 13`

What is the main idea of the lecture?

(A) Ways to change the light in a sun set

(B) Everyday places that a prism changes light

Note-taking

B. Read the full passage. Then listen to the full lecture. Take notes in the boxes below. `Track 14`

Prisms

Have you ever experimented with a prism? It is a great way to understand more about colors and light.

The first thing a prism does is refract light. This means that it changes the direction of the light as it passes through the prism. Light travels in waves. When light goes into the prism, it looks like plain white light.

The next thing the prism does is bend the waves of light. When the light goes out the other side, it is split into many different colors. These colors always appear in the same pattern. This pattern is called a spectrum. The color spectrum is composed of red, orange, yellow, green, blue, indigo, and violet.

Reading

Main idea: A prism's effect _____
Key points:
- A prism _____
- A prism bends the _____

Lecture

Main idea: Everyday places that a _____
Key points:
- Can see it in the colors _____
  - The atmosphere scatters _____
- Plain white light enters each raindrop
  - The raindrop acts like a _____
  - This is how a _____

C. Read the prompt.

Summarize the main points made in the lecture and explain how they support the main points in the reading passage.

D. Fill in the blanks of the sample response using phrases from the box. Use your notes to help you.

The reading explains how a prism _____ light. White light is changed as it goes through a prism. This causes the colors of the rainbow to come out the other side of the prism. The lecture explains how we can see this every day.

The speaker says that the _____ the blue light in the sky to make the sunset look red, yellow, and orange. The speaker also explains that a rainbow is the result of _____ acting like a prism. A prism takes _____ and turns it into many beautiful colors.

a raindrop	refracts and bends
atmosphere scatters	plain light

E. Fill in the blanks with the correct words.

composed	experiment	plain	scattered	waves

1. A children's volcano _____ requires using baking soda, vinegar, and lots of mud.
2. Radio _____ travel through the air.
3. Surprisingly, the most popular ice cream flavor is still _____ vanilla.
4. A basic essay is usually _____ of an introduction, body, and conclusion.
5. When light shines through a window, dust can be seen _____ everywhere.

Test

Step 1

Read the passage. Then listen to a lecture. Take notes in the boxes below. **Track 15**

The Color Spectrum

There are two types of light in the color spectrum. Plain white light is what our eyes can see. When it is refracted, we see the same color pattern. The pattern can be seen through experimenting with prisms. It is also the seven-color pattern seen in rainbows. There are many colors in the spectrum. However, our eyes can only see certain ones. The spectrum is composed of other types of light. Human eyes cannot see them. An example of this is sunburn. You cannot see the light that caused the burn. However, your skin knows it is real!

Reading

Main idea: The color spectrum has _____
Key points:
- Plain _____
- Other types of light cannot be seen by _____
  - An example is the light that causes _____

Lecture

Main idea: There are types of light that _____
Key points:
- The spectrum is composed of _____
- Humans can see about a million different _____
  - Some women _____
- Humans cannot see _____
  - Birds and _____

Step 2

Read and listen to the prompt. **Track 16**

Summarize the main points made in the lecture and explain how they support the main points in the reading passage.

Step 3

Complete the outline using your notes from Step 1.

Topic: The reading and the lecture are about the different types of light.

A. The reading discusses the two types of light in _____
    1. Humans can only see _____
    2. There are other types of light that the _____
       • The light that causes _____

B. The lecture discusses how the spectrum is composed of _____
    1. The average person can see about _____
       • Some women can see _____
    2. Humans cannot see ultra-violet light but _____

Conclusion: The lecture supports the points made in the reading by giving examples
          of what light humans can and cannot see.

Step 4

Complete the response using your outline from Step 3.

    The reading and the lecture are _____.
The reading discusses _____.
Humans can only see _____. However, there are many
_____.
    The lecture supports the reading by giving further information. The lecture discusses
how the spectrum is _____. However, the average person
can only _____.
The speaker also gives an example of light that humans cannot see. This is _____
_____.
    The lecture supports the points _____
_____.

Check-up

Fill in the blanks with the correct words.

motion	spectrum	aloud	pattern	mumble	prism

1. A piece of crystal can be a _____ that bends light into colors.
2. A thought is something you do not say _____.
3. A rainbow shows all the colors in the _____.
4. The _____ of a car makes some people sick.
5. It's important not to _____ when giving a presentation.
6. Each leopard has a unique spotted _____ on its fur.

[05] Independent

Getting Ready to Write

A. Learn the words.

Key Vocabulary

easily	without difficulties
program	a set of computer instructions that make a computer perform certain functions
spam	unwanted email

TOEFL® Vocabulary

reach	to contact
download	to get from the Internet
software	a computer program
deal with	to solve a problem
stress	a feeling of worry, pressure, or nervousness

B. Read the prompt. Then answer the questions.

Describe an experience you had with a computer recently.

1. What was the experience?
   The experience was _____.

2. Why did you need to use the computer?
   I needed to use the computer because _____.

3. Could you have done this activity without your computer?
   I _____.

4. Do you think this experience was easier because of the computer?
   I think that _____.

Practice

A. Read the question.

Do you agree or disagree with the following statement?

Computers have made people's lives better.

Use specific reasons and examples to support your answer.

Sample Response 1

B. Read the sample response. Then answer the question.

I do not think that computers have made people's lives better. Sometimes they make them worse. First, computers add stress to our lives. People get a lot of spam that they do not want to read. It can take a lot of time to delete spam. My dad says that this wastes a lot of his company's money. Also, computers can break. They can be expensive to fix. Computers cost a lot of money and do not always work. My computer at home sometimes turns itself off for no reason. I have lost my homework before when it turned off. Therefore, I think that computers just cause too much stress.

Which side of the statement does the response take?
(A) Agree   (B) Disagree

Outline

C. Complete the outline for the response.

Topic: Computers _____ made people's better.
A. Computers add _____
   1. People get a lot of _____
   2. Spam wastes company's _____
B. Computers can break and be _____
   1. Computers cost a lot of money and _____
   2. I have lost _____
Conclusion: Computers just _____.

D. Underline the transitional words or phrases in the sample response.

Sample Response 2

E. Read the sample response. Then answer the question.

I think that computers have made our lives better. To begin, people can communicate easily through email. I can send messages online to reach my friends who live far away. Sending a letter would take a long time. Also, I think that the Internet has made it easier to do many things. People can find information. They can download programs to help them. I use the Internet to help with my homework. I can find help when I am confused about math problems. I also use software to write essays. I do not like dealing with spam. Still, I know computers have made my life better.

Which side of the statement does the response take?

(A) Agree   (B) Disagree

Outline

F. Complete the outline for the response.

Topic: Computers have made our _____.
A. Computers let people _____
   1. Can send messages to friends who _____
   2. Sending letters takes a _____
B. The Internet makes it _____
   1. People can find _____ and download _____
   2. I use the _____ for homework, and _____ for essays.
Conclusion: Computers have _____.

G. Underline the transitional words or phrases in the sample response.

TOEFL® Vocabulary Practice

H. Fill in the blanks with the correct words.

reach	download	software	deal with	stress

1. The telephone was an invention that let people _____ each other over long distances.

2. Doctors have to _____ complex medical problems every day.

3. The Internet now lets us _____ music for a small price.

4. You can get _____ for your computer that lets you write letters and essays.

5. Having too much to do is a leading cause of _____.

Test

Step 1

Read the question.

Do you agree or disagree with the following statement?

Computers have made people's lives better.

Use specific reasons and examples to support your answer.

Step 2

State your opinion.

I _____ with the statement.

Step 3

Write an outline for your essay that will support your opinion.

Topic: I _____ computers have made people's lives better.

A. _____

    1. _____

    2. _____

B. _____

    1. _____

    2. _____

Conclusion: Without computers, _____.

Step 4

Complete the response using your outline from above.

I _____ computers have made peoples' lives better.

I think this because _____.

For instance, _____

_____.

I also think this because _____.

For example, _____

_____.

Without computers, _____.

Integrated - Business

Getting Ready to Write

A. Learn the words.

tried-and-true	proven to be good
costly	expensive
accident	something that happens unexpectedly and often results in harm or damage

right	the permission to do or have something
joint	shared by two or more people
contract	a formal written decision between two people or parties
benefit	an advantage given
profit	money leftover after paying business costs

Reading Passage

B. Read the first part of a passage. Then answer the questions.

A Franchise

A franchise is a business. It is when one company gives another the right to sell its products. These companies have to have a joint contract. This gives out the right to use the company name.

There are many benefits to owning a franchise. The first is that they can help owners save money.

---

1. What is the main idea of the passage?

   (A) The benefits of franchise businesses

   (B) The types of franchise businesses

2. What do you think the rest of the passage and the lecture will talk about? Write two or three ideas below.

   _____

   _____

Practice

Lecture

A. Listen to the first part of a lecture. Then answer the question. `Track 17`

What is the main idea of the lecture?

(A) Definition of a franchise

(B) Disadvantages of running a franchise

Note-taking

B. Read the full passage. Then listen to the full lecture. Take notes in the boxes below. `Track 18`

A Franchise

A franchise is a business. It is when one company gives another the right to sell its products. These companies have to have a joint contract. This gives out the right to use the company name.

There are many benefits to owning a franchise. The first is that they can help owners save money. They use tried-and-true business ideas. So, a new owner will not have to make costly mistakes. Owners can usually start making profits right away. The second is that franchises give owners lots of freedom of choice. Deciding which franchise to choose is the hard part.

Reading

Main idea: The benefits of owning _____
Key points:
- A franchise can help owners save _____
- Franchises give owners lots of _____

Lecture

Main idea: The problems with opening _____
Key points:
- Franchise owners have to pay a _____
- In franchises, there is no _____
  - Doing so would break the _____

C. Read the prompt.

Summarize the main points made in the lecture and explain how they refute the main points in the reading passage.

Sample Response

D. Fill in the blanks of the sample response using phrases from the box. Use your notes to help you.

The reading explains how a franchise business allows one company to _____ of another company through a joint contract. A franchise can help _____ save money and have freedom of choice.

The lecture, however, describes some problems of opening a franchise business. The speaker says that the franchise fee makes _____ very expensive. Unlike what the reading says, the speaker also says that there is no freedom to _____. If something is wrong, the franchise owner won't let the business owner change anything. This can make it very difficult to be successful.

opening the business	change things
sell the products	business owners

TOEFL® Vocabulary Practice

E. Fill in the blanks with the correct words.

right	joint	contract	benefit	profit

1. Athletes _____ from a lot of training.
2. Criminals have the _____ to have a fair trial.
3. A company's owners have meetings to reach a _____ agreement.
4. Musicians who become part of a record company have to sign a _____.
5. A restaurant's largest goal is to make a _____.

Test

Step 1

Read the passage. Then listen to the lecture. Take notes in the boxes below. **Track 19**

Types of Franchises

There are two types of franchises. They both offer a famous name as a main benefit. The first is called a product-and-trade-name franchise. This is a contract that allows the owner to make or sell a well-known product. The owner can then profit from selling a product with a name most people recognize. Car dealerships are this type of franchise. So are tire dealers.

The second type is called a business-format franchise. These provide the owner with the right to use a well-known name. Plus, they provide a tried-and-true system for running the business. Most fast-food restaurants and hotels are this type.

Reading

Main idea: The benefits of two _____
Key points:
  • A product-and-trade-name franchise allows the owner to _____
  • A business-format franchise gives the owner the _____

Lecture

Main idea: A well-known name can _____
Key points:
  • One bad product can _____
    - Accidents were caused by _____
    - Store owners lost _____
  • Business mistakes made by one business can hurt _____
    - Children died from eating _____
    - Thousands of owners lost _____

Step 2

Read and listen to the prompt. **Track 20**

Summarize the main points made in the lecture and explain how they refute the main points in the reading passage.

Step 3

Complete the outline using your notes from Step 1.

Topic: The reading and the lecture are about how a well-known name can either help or hurt a business.
A. The reading discusses the benefits of
  1. product-and-_____
  2. business-_____
B. The lecture discusses how selling a well-known name or product can _____
  1. Goodyear _____
    • They caused _____
  2. Jack in _____
    • A few sold _____
  3. The owners lost _____
Conclusion: The lecture refutes the points made in the reading about the benefits of a brand name.

Step 4

Complete the response using your outline from Step 3.

The reading and the lecture are about _____
_____.
The reading discusses the benefits of _____
_____.
They both offer benefits of well-known brand names or products.
  The lecture refutes the reading by discussing how _____
_____.
Examples included Goodyear tires that _____
and a few Jack in the Box restaurants that _____.
In both these cases, the owners of business that sold _____
because they were selling a well-known brand.
  Therefore, the lecture _____
_____.

Check-up

Fill in the blanks with the correct words.

easily	program	spam	tried-and-true	costly	accidents

1. There are more than 11 million _____ on US roads every year.

2. Some people receive over 200 _____ messages every day.

3. Making a movie is a very _____ process, but one that can be very profitable.

4. A metal detector can _____ find a lost coin, even if it is in deep grass.

5. Suntan lotion is a _____ way to protect your skin from the sun's harsh rays.

6. A word processor is a computer _____ that allows the user to write using a keyboard.

[06] Independent

Getting Ready to Write

A. Learn the words.

Key Vocabulary	
useful	helpful
hopefully	believing good will come
principal	the supervisor of a school

TOEFL® Vocabulary	
continually	over and over again
remark	a comment
improve	to make better
fault	a weakness or flaw
evaluate	to measure or test ability

B. Read the prompt. Then answer the questions.

Describe a time when you felt you received an unfair grade for work that you did.

1. What was the experience?
   The experience was _____.

2. Why did you feel the grade was unfair?
   I felt this way because _____.

3. Did you take any action?
   Yes, I did/No, I didn't because _____.

4. What did you learn from the experience?
   I learned _____.

Practice

A. Read the question.

Do you agree or disagree with the following statement?

Students should grade their teachers.

Use specific reasons and examples to support your answer.

Sample Response 1

B. Read the sample response. Then answer the question.

I think that students should grade their teachers. I feel this would be useful for two reasons. First of all, some teachers have been teaching for a long time. They are used to continually doing things the same old ways. Low grades or bad remarks from their students would help them. They would see that they need to improve. If no one graded them, they would not have to look at their faults. They would keep doing the same old things. Second, this process would allow some teachers to know how much they are appreciated. Students do not often thank their teachers for their hard work. Giving high grades to teachers who do a good job could be a good way to do this. Hopefully, grading teachers would be something that was good for everyone.

Which side of the statement does the response take?
(A) Agree   (B) Disagree

Outline

C. Complete the outline for the response.

Topic: Students _____ grade their teachers.
A. Some teachers have been teaching for a _____
   1. Teachers are used to _____
   2. Bad grades would help them _____
B. Teachers could see how much they are _____
   1. Students don't _____
   2. Giving _____
Conclusion: Hopefully, grading teachers would be _____
_____.

D. Underline the transitional words or phrases in the sample response.

E. Read the sample response. Then answer the question.

I do not think that teachers should be graded by their students. I feel this way for two reasons. First, teachers have already been to school. They have studied and received grades. They were shown how to teach. They could not teach now if they had not passed. Second, there is already a type of grading system for teachers. The principal of the school checks that teachers are good at their job. He or she evaluates them every year. The principal has much more experience in grading than students do. That is why I do not believe that students should grade their teachers.

Which side of the statement does the response take?

(A) Agree   (B) Disagree

Outline

F. Complete the outline for the response.

Topic: Students _____ grade their teachers.

  A. Teachers have already _____

     1. They were _____

     2. They could not teach if they _____

  B. There is already a grading _____

     1. Principal checks that they _____

     2. Principal evaluates them _____

     3. Principal has more _____

Conclusion: I do not believe _____.

G. Underline the transitional words or phrases in the sample response.

TOEFL® Vocabulary Practice

H. Fill in the blanks with the correct words.

continually	evaluate	fault	improve	remark

1. Putting off homework is a common _____ of many students.

2. Scientists _____ many things when testing a theory.

3. It is not polite to make a loud _____ during a movie.

4. Coaches want their players to _____ their skills.

5. It's a good trait to _____ want to learn new things.

Test

Step 1

Read the question.

Do you agree or disagree with the following statement?

Students should grade their teachers.

Use specific reasons and examples to support your answer.

Step 2

State your opinion.

I _____ with the statement.

Step 3

Write an outline for your essay that will support your opinion.

Topic: I think that teachers _____.
A. _____
    1. _____
    2. _____
B. _____
    1. _____
    2. _____
Conclusion: I think that teachers _____.

Step 4

Complete the response using your outline from above.

I think _____ be graded.
This is because _____.
For example, _____
_____.

I also think that _____.
This would help _____
_____.

For these reasons, I think that teachers _____.

Integrated - Astronomy

Getting Ready to Write

A. Learn the words.

Key Vocabulary

trap	to catch something and keep it in a particular place
gravitational	relating to gravity, which is a force that pulls things down
pull	a force that brings things to itself

TOEFL® Vocabulary

theory	a set of ideas that explain something
explanation	a reason given to help someone understand something
mass	a piece or amount that has no definite size or shape
claim	to declare that something is true
rate	the speed of something moving

Reading Passage

B. Read the first part of a passage. Then answer the questions.

> **The Fission Theory**
>
> The Fission Theory was introduced in 1879. It was an early explanation about how the moon was formed. It was based on two ideas.
> First, scientists thought the moon was made from a piece of the Earth.

1. What is the main idea of the passage?

   (A) A new theory about how the moon was formed

   (B) An early theory about how the moon was formed

2. What do you think the rest of the passage and the lecture will talk about? Write two or three ideas below.

   _____

   _____

Practice

Lecture

A. Listen to the first part of a lecture. Then answer the question. `Track 21`

What is the main idea of the lecture?

(A) Evidence that supports a theory

(B) Evidence against a theory

Note-taking

B. Read the full passage. Then listen to the full lecture. Take notes in the boxes below. `Track 22`

The Fission Theory

The Fission Theory was introduced in 1879. It was an early explanation about how the moon was formed. It was based on two ideas.

First, scientists thought the moon was made from a piece of the Earth. They claimed it came from a huge piece of earth where the Pacific Ocean now is.

Second, they thought that the Earth was spinning at a very fast rate. That's the reason it threw off this large piece. They believed this huge piece became trapped in the Earth's gravitational pull. Then it began orbiting the Earth as the moon.

Reading

Main idea: The fission theory explains how _____
Key points:
- The moon was _____
  - It came from _____
- The Earth was spinning so fast it threw off the _____
  - It began orbiting _____

Lecture

Main idea: The fission theory does not _____
Key points:
- The rocks from the ocean and the moon are _____
- The Earth couldn't have spun fast _____

C. Read the prompt.

Summarize the main points made in the lecture and explain how they challenge the main points in the reading passage.

Sample Response

D. Fill in the blanks of the sample response using phrases from the box. Use your notes to help you.

The reading discusses how _____ was the first to explain how the moon was formed. It stated that a piece of the Earth broke off and was pulled into the _____. This piece became the moon.

The lecture explains how this theory does not make sense today. The speaker says the rocks from the _____ and the rocks on the moon are made of different chemicals.

The speaker also says that the Earth could not have _____ for a piece to break off and be pulled into orbit. If the moon was joined to the Earth, it would still spin too slowly for a piece to be thrown off.

Earth's orbit	spun fast enough
The Fission Theory	Pacific Ocean

TOEFL® Vocabulary Practice

E. Fill in the blanks with the correct words.

claims	explanation	mass	rate	theory

1. A teacher usually wants a(n) _____ from a student who is always late.
2. A person doesn't have to be a scientist to develop a _____ about something.
3. Police will write you a ticket if you are driving at a high _____ of speed.
4. Scientific _____ cannot always be proven to be true.
5. A large _____ moving in space may be a meteor.

Test

Step 1

Read the passage. Then listen to the lecture. Take notes in the boxes below. `Track 23`

The Moon

If you look at the moon, you can see dark spots on it. These are moon craters. Long ago, people believed the theory that these were made by volcanoes. They believed this explanation for two reasons.

First of all, they thought the dark spots were made out of lava. In fact, much of the surface area on the moon is covered by cooled lava.

Second, the moon has volcano domes. These are the mountain-like hills. The volcanoes on the moon are smaller than the ones on the Earth. They stopped erupting a long time ago. However, scientists once claimed the early eruptions made the craters.

Reading

Main idea: People believed that volcanoes _____
Key points:
- Dark spots were made of _____
- Moon's _____
- Moon has volcano _____

Lecture

Main idea: Reasons why the volcano _____
Key points:
- The craters are _____
- Volcanoes don't leave _____
  - Now they think meteorites _____
- The craters are older _____
  - The volcanoes formed _____

Step 2

Read and listen to the prompt. `Track 24`

Summarize the main points made in the lecture and explain how they challenge the main points in the reading passage.

Step 3

Complete the outline using your notes from Step 1.

Topic: The reading and the lecture discuss theories on how the moon's craters were formed.

A. The reading says that volcanoes formed _____
   1. Hardened lava made _____
   2. The moon has lots of _____
B. The lecture says that volcanoes don't make _____
   1. The craters were made by _____
   2. The craters are older _____
      • The volcanoes were formed _____

Conclusion: The lecture challenges the reading by showing how volcanoes could not have formed the craters on the moon.

Step 4

Complete the sample response using your outline from Step 3.

The reading and the lecture discuss _____
_____.
    The reading says that hardened lava from volcanoes was once thought to have formed _____. The reading also says that people thought this because _____.
    The lecture discusses why the volcano theory is not correct. In the lecture, the speaker says _____
_____.
The speaker also says that the craters are older _____
_____.
    The lecture challenges the reading by _____
_____.

Check-up

Fill in the blanks with the correct words.

gravitational	pulls	trap	hopefully	principal	useful

1. The school _____ is the supervisor of every teacher.
2. A spider builds a web to _____ insects.
3. Studying is a _____ thing to do before a test.
4. The sun's _____ pull keeps the planets in orbit around it.
5. Many children look _____ at their parents when they see something they want to buy.
6. The first car on a train _____ the rest of them.

[Review 1]

Step 1

Read the question.

Do you agree or disagree with the following statement?

Boys and girls should go to different schools.

Use specific reasons and examples to support your answer.

Step 2

State your opinion.

I _____ with the statement.

Step 3

Write an outline for your essay that will support your opinion.

Topic: Boys and girls _____ go to different schools.
A. _____
    1. _____
    2. _____
B. _____
    1. _____
    2. _____
Conclusion: Boys and girls should _____.

Step 4

Complete the response using your outline from above.

I think that boys and girls should _____.
I think this because _____.
I think that _____
_____.
I also believe that _____.
For example, _____
_____.
These are the reasons I think that _____
_____.

Step 1

🎧 Read the passage. Then listen to the lecture. Take notes in the boxes below. `Track 25`

Constellations

The sky is divided into eighty-eight areas called constellations. The constellations are groups of stars and have names. The stars appear to form perfect shapes in the sky. There are so many stars that it is hard to remember where they all are. The constellations' names help people remember. Constellations move at a slow rate. In our era, they will always be found in about the same place at the same time of the year.

Many constellations were given names describing what their shapes looked like. The best known is the Big Dipper. It is not actually a constellation. It is part of the constellation Ursa Major. It is also known as Great Bear. Big Dipper is the name adopted in North America. This grouping of stars has continually been seen for hundreds of years.

Reading

Main idea: Constellations are groups of _____
Key points:
- It is hard to remember where _____
- They will be found in the same place at the _____
- They were given names describing what their _____

Lecture

Main idea: Constellations are helpful for remembering _____
Key points:
- The stories are an explanation as to where these "pictures" _____
- These legends were useful to _____
  - In some places the seasons _____
  - Constellations appear at the _____
  - Farmers would know it was time for _____
- This dependence on the sky became _____

Step 2

🎧 Read and listen to the prompt. `Track 26`

Summarize the main points made in the lecture, and explain how they support the main points in the reading passage.

Step 3

Complete the outline using your notes from Step 1.

Topic: The reading and the lecture are about why the constellations have names.

A. The reading discusses why they have _____

    1. The names help _____

    2. The names were descriptions of what they _____

B. The lecture discusses how constellations have _____

C. The reading says that the constellations will be seen _____

D. The speaker says some places have _____

    1. Farmers used constellations to decide when to _____

    2. Cultures are dependent on _____

Conclusion: The lecture supports the points made in the reading about why naming constellations was important.

Step 4

Complete the sample response using your outline from Step 3.

>   The reading and the lecture are _____.
> The reading discusses that they have names to _____
> _____.
> The lecture supports this by discussing how constellations have _____
> _____.
> The reading also says that the constellations will be seen _____.
>   The speaker supports the reading by explaining how some places have
> _____. Therefore, farmers used constellations to
> _____.
> This was an example of how many cultures are _____.
>   The lecture supports _____
> _____.

Step 1

🎧 **Read the passage. Then listen to the lecture. Take notes in the boxes below.** `Track 27`

World War II

Over the course of six years, World War II spread around the Earth. It affected many people. In all, more than fifty countries were directly involved in the war. There were two groups, the Allies and the Axis. In 1941, the Japanese were part of the Axis and they attacked US forces. This happened at Pearl Harbor. The US response was to join the Allies to fight the Axis. In 1945, the US dropped atomic bombs on the cities of Hiroshima and Nagasaki. The Axis eventually surrendered.

It was not just the US and Japan that were affected. There were huge social and economic effects for all.

Reading

Main idea: How World War II spread around _____

Key points:
- Fifty countries were _____
- Japan attacked U.S. forces at _____
- US dropped atomic bombs on _____
- There were huge social and economic _____

Lecture

Main idea: World War II is the most tragic war humanity _____

Key points:
- The Holocaust was one of the most severe _____
- Almost six million Jews were _____
  - Nazis were _____
- This was the most _____
  - Major cities had been _____
  - Supplies of all kinds had been _____
- The situation took a long time _____

Step 2

🎧 **Read and listen to the prompt.** `Track 28`

Summarize the main points made in the lecture, and explain how they support the main points in the reading passage.

Step 3

Complete the outline using your notes from Step 1.

Topic: The reading and the lecture are about the effects of World War II.

A. The reading discussed how it _____

   1. The Japanese _____

   2. The Americans dropped atomic _____

B. Other people also suffered social and _____

C. The speaker says that WWII was a _____

   1. The holocaust

   2. Almost six million Jews were murdered by _____

D. WWII was _____

   1. Cities were _____

   2. Supplies had _____

E. It took a long _____

Conclusion: The lecture supports the points made in the reading by giving other social and economic effects of World War II.

Step 4

Complete the response using your outline from Step 3.

The reading and the lecture are _____.
The reading discusses how it _____
_____.
The Japanese attacked _____
_____.
However, the reading says that other people also suffered social and _____
_____.
The speaker supports this by saying that World War II _____
and that in the holocaust almost six million Jews _____.
This was a social effect. The speaker also supports the reading by discussing the economic effects. World War II was the most expensive war ever because cities
_____.
The lecture supports _____
_____.

Step 1

Read the question.

Do you agree or disagree with the following statement?

Friends are more important than family.

Use specific reasons and examples to support your answer.

Step 2

State your opinion.

I _____ with the statement.

Step 3

Write an outline for your essay that will support your opinion.

Topic: _____ more important than _____.
A. _____
    1. _____
    2. _____
B. _____
    1. _____
    2. _____
Conclusion: I think that _____ more important.

Step 4

Complete the response using your outline from above.

I think that _____.
First, I think this because _____.
For example, _____
_____.
Secondly, _____.
For example, _____
_____.
These are the reasons I think that _____.

[07] Independent

Getting Ready to Write

A. Learn the words.

Key Vocabulary

frightened	to feel afraid
comfort	to make someone feel better
natural	normal; expected

TOEFL® Vocabulary

trust	to believe someone is right or good
crisis	a very bad or stressful event
counselor	a person who helps people talk about problems
private	alone; away from other people
emotion	a strong feeling

B. Read the prompt. Then answer the questions.

Describe a time when someone in your family cried.

1. What was the reason the person cried?
   The reason was _____.

2. How did you feel?
   I felt _____.

3. What did others in your family say?
   Others in my family said _____.

4. How do you think the person who cried felt afterward?
   I think that _____.

Practice

A. Read the question.

Do you agree or disagree with the following statement?

Parents should not cry in front of their children.

Use specific reasons and examples to support your answer.

Sample Response 1

B. Read the sample response. Then answer the question.

I think parents should not cry in front of their kids. They should never do it. Why is it a bad idea? Well, here are two reasons. First of all, it scares little kids. Children trust their parents. They want their parents to protect them. If their parents cry in front of them, they are frightened. They do not feel safe. They think something terrible has happened. Second, kids should not know about bad problems. Parents often cry because of a crisis. They might cry because someone has died or has lost a job. Young children cannot understand these things. It is better if they do not know about them. Therefore, parents should never cry in front of their kids. They should go to a counselor if they need to express their feelings. Or, they should cry in private.

Which side of the statement does the response take?
(A) Agree   (B) Disagree

Outline

C. Complete the outline for the response.

Topic: Parents _____ cry in front of their children.
A. It scares _____
    1. They want their parents to _____
    2. They will be _____
    3. They will think something _____
B. Kids should not know about _____
    1. Parents cry because of _____
    2. Kids cannot _____
Conclusion: Instead, parents should _____.

D. Underline the transitional words or phrases in the sample response.

E. Read the sample response. Then answer the question.

I think parents should cry in front of their children. It is a good thing sometimes. Here are two reasons why. First, it is healthy to share emotions. Parents need to express emotions. It will make them feel better. The kids will see that it is all right to feel sad sometimes. It is all right for them to cry, too. Second, it can help parents and kids feel closer together. The parents can explain why they are sad. Kids can respond to their parents. They can comfort their parents. Kids and parents can talk about their problems. They can solve them together. So, I think it is natural for parents to cry in front of their children sometimes. They should not feel bad about it. There is nothing wrong with it.

Which side of the statement does the response take?

(A) Agree   (B) Disagree

Outline

F. Complete the outline for the response.

Topic: Parents _____ cry in front of their children.
A. It's healthy for parents to _____
   1. Parents will feel _____
   2. Kids will see that it is all right to _____
B. Parents and kids can feel _____
   1. Kids can _____
   2. Kids and parents can _____
Conclusion: I think _____.

G. Underline the transitional words or phrases in the sample response.

TOEFL® Vocabulary Practice

H. Fill in the blanks with the correct words.

counselor	private	crisis	emotion	trust

1. A _____ person does not feel comfortable sharing emotions with others.
2. Many schools have at least one _____ who can help students deal with their problems.
3. Happiness, sadness, fear, joy, hate, and love are all examples of _____.
4. A solid friendship should be built on _____.
5. Many people go to counseling when dealing with a personal _____.

Test

Step 1

Read the question.

> **Do you agree or disagree with the following statement?**
>
> Parents should not cry in front of their children.
>
> **Use specific reasons and examples to support your answer.**

Step 2

State your opinion.

I _____ with the statement.

Step 3

Write an outline for your essay that will support your opinion.

Topic: I think that parents _____ cry in front of their children.
A. _____
   1. _____
   2. _____
B. _____
   1. _____
   2. _____
Conclusion: I feel parents _____ cry in front of their children.

Step 4

Complete the response using your outline from above.

I think that parents _____ cry in front of their children.
I think this because _____.
For example, _____
_____.

I also believe this because _____.
For example, _____
_____.
This is why I feel parents _____ cry in front of their children.

Integrated - Literature

Getting Ready to Write

A. Learn the words.

Key Vocabulary

wise	having a lot of knowledge
terrible	very bad; awful
speak out	to offer an opinion in public

TOEFL® Vocabulary

genre	a type or category of something
author	a person who has written a book
admire	to respect and like someone
courage	the ability to do the right thing in a difficult situation
awareness	an understanding of a situation or subject

Reading Passage

B. Read the first part of a passage. Then answer the questions.

> **Autobiographies**
>
> A biography is a true story. It is written about someone's life. Some people write about their own lives. These books are called autobiographies. They belong to a special genre. They help us get to know a person's feelings. The author talks about his or her life.

1. What is the main idea of the passage?

   (A) Comparing two different genres of autobiographies

   (B) Explaining why autobiographies are important

2. What do you think the rest of the passage and the lecture will talk about? Write two or three ideas below.

   _____

   _____

Practice

Lecture

A. Listen to the first part of a lecture. Then answer the question. `Track 29`

What is the main idea of the lecture?

(A) Explaining why people like autobiographies

(B) Showing effects of an autobiography

Note-taking

B. Read the full passage. Then listen to the full lecture. Take notes in the boxes below. `Track 30`

Autobiographies

A biography is a true story. It is written about someone's life. Some people write about their own lives. These books are called autobiographies. They belong to a special genre. They help us get to know a person's feelings. The author talks about his or her life. People often admire the author. It is like meeting a wise friend.

Autobiographies also help solve problems. Some people write about their problems and their courage. Readers feel sad about these problems. They want to solve them. That is why autobiographies are important. They help us understand other people. They inspire us to make things better.

Reading

Main idea: Autobiographies are books people write about _____
Key points:
- We can understand the author's _____
- Autobiographies also teach us about _____
- Autobiographies inspire us to _____

Lecture

Main idea: Frederick Douglass wrote an autobiography that helped _____
Key points:
- He was a slave, but he _____
- The autobiography helped raise people's _____
- The autobiography also _____

C. Read the prompt.

Summarize the main points made in the lecture and explain how they support the main points in the reading passage.

Sample Response

D. Fill in the blanks of the sample response using phrases from the box. Use your notes to help you.

The reading explains what an autobiography is and why this genre is important. One reason is that people are _____ the author's courage. Another reason is that these books teach us about problems.

The lecture illustrates how an autobiography _____ in the United States. The speaker says that Frederick Douglass wrote his autobiography after he _____. The speaker says that many people read his book and it made them think about slavery. The speaker also explains that it gave other _____. They began to speak out about their problems.

inspired by   helped end slavery
escaped from slavery   slaves courage

TOEFL® Vocabulary Practice

E. Fill in the blanks with the correct words.

genre	awareness	author	courage	admire

1. Many students _____ their teachers because they are very intelligent.
2. The media increases the public's _____ of problems in the world.
3. Bookstores organize their books by the name of the _____.
4. People who escaped from slavery had a lot of _____.
5. Classical is just one type of musical _____.

Test

Step 1

🎧 Read the passage. Then listen to the lecture. Take notes in the boxes below. **Track 31**

Memoirs

A memoir is a kind of book. It is about a time in someone's life. A memoir is not the same as an autobiography. It is a different genre.

First, a memoir is usually about a certain time in a person's life. It is not about their whole life. It is just about a short time.

Second, memoirs are often about major events. Authors write about wars or elections. They usually know a lot about the event. They speak out and say what it was like to live through it. However, it is more about the event. It is not just about how the person felt. Memoirs are a kind of history. They can be very interesting.

Reading

Main idea: A memoir is a book about a time _____
Key points:
- It is about a certain time in a person's life, not _____
- It is usually about a major event the person _____
- It talks about a _____

Lecture

Main idea: Anne Frank wrote a famous memoir about _____
Key points:
- Her family had to hide and she wrote _____
- It tells about the terrible things _____
- Many people think she was very wise and they admire _____
- Many people learn about _____

Step 2

🎧 Read and listen to the prompt. **Track 32**

Summarize the main points made in the lecture and explain how they support the main points in the reading passage.

Step 3

Complete the outline using your notes from Step 1.

Topic: The reading and the lecture are about how a memoir can help people learn about history.

A. The reading says memoirs are _____

    1. They are about a certain _____

    2. They usually focus on a major _____

B. The lecture discusses a famous memoir that Anne _____

    1. Her family was in hiding during _____

    2. She told about the terrible things that _____

    3. People think she is wise and _____

    4. It also teaches _____

_____

Conclusion: The lecture supports the points made in the reading about memoirs by giving a famous example of a memoir from World War II.

Step 4

Complete the response using your outline from Step 3.

    The reading and the lecture are _____.

The reading says that memoirs _____.

The reading also says that memoirs usually focus on _____.

    The lecture then discusses a famous memoir Anne Frank wrote when _____

_____.

In the lecture, the speaker explains that Anne Frank told about _____

_____.

People think she is _____.

It also teaches about _____.

    The lecture supports the _____

_____.

Check-up

Fill in the blanks with the correct words.

terrible	natural	comfort	frightened	speak out	wise

1. The _____ storm left the entire city without power or water.

2. A person who reads about history will probably become very _____.

3. After being in a serious car accident, people are often too _____ to drive.

4. Family members should always _____ one another.

5. US citizens who are displeased with their government often _____ about it.

6. It is only _____ to feel unhappy sometimes.

[08] Independent

Getting Ready to Write

A. Learn the words.

Key Vocabulary

adventure	an exciting event
mystery	something that is not known
giggle	to laugh in a childish or silly way

TOEFL® Vocabulary

abundant	numerous; in large quantities
amuse	to bring laughter or joy
bother	to put forth effort
retire	to stop working at an older age
throughout	to occur in every part of something

B. Read the prompt. Then answer the questions.

Describe an experience when you spent time with someone much older than you.

1. What was the experience?
   It was _____.

2. Why did you do this?
   I did this because _____.

3. How did you feel about spending time with him/her/them?
   I felt _____.

4. What do you think the other person/people felt about their experience?
   I think that _____.

Practice

A. Read the question.

Do you agree or disagree with the following statement?

Old people have more fun than young people.

Use specific reasons and examples to support your answer.

Sample Response 1

B. Read the sample response. Then answer the question.

I feel that young people have more fun than old people. First, I think this because younger people are always looking for an adventure. They like to solve mysteries. They like to learn new things. Older people are happy just relaxing. They talk about what they used to do. Second, young people also laugh more. Laughter is abundant wherever young people are. When there are older people around, it is usually quiet. Young people seem more amused with things that happen. Older people just act like they have seen it all. I believe older people don't want to bother with fun.

Which side of the statement does the response take?

(A) Agree   (B) Disagree

Outline

C. Complete the outline for the response.

Topic: Young people _____ fun than old people.
A. Young people look for _____
   1. Young people like to solve _____
   2. Old people just want to _____
B. Young people _____
   1. Young people are more _____
   2. Old people have _____
Conclusion: I believe _____.

D. Underline the transitional words or phrases in the sample response.

E. Read the sample response. Then answer the question.

I believe that older people have more fun than younger people. I think this because my grandmother is more fun than a lot of my friends. She giggles about funny things. She likes to tell jokes and make people laugh. She is retired and takes many trips because she doesn't have to work. Also, older people tell good stories. They have lived a long time and have learned so many things. They can tell you about exciting adventures they had throughout their lives. For these reasons, I cannot wait to be older. I am ready to have more fun.

Which side of the statement does the response take?

(A) Agree   (B) Disagree

Outline

F. Complete the outline for the response.

Topic: Older people _____ fun than younger people.
A. Grandmother is more _____
   1. She tells _____
   2. She is _____
B. Older people tell _____
   1. They have _____
   2. They can tell you about exciting _____
Conclusion: I cannot wait to be _____.

G. Underline the transitional words or phrases in the sample response.

TOEFL® Vocabulary Practice

H. Fill in the blanks with the correct words.

amuse	abundant	bother	throughout	retire

1. Most countries have had many rulers _____ history.

2. Pumpkins are _____ in the fall.

3. Children read comic books to _____ themselves.

4. Younger siblings sometimes like to _____ their older siblings.

5. People often enjoy traveling a lot after they _____.

Test

Step 1

Read the question.

Do you agree or disagree with the following statement?

Old people have more fun than young people.

Use specific reasons and examples to support your answer.

Step 2

State your opinion.

I _____ with the statement.

Step 3

Write an outline for your essay that will support your opinion.

Topic: I think that _____ have more fun than _____.

A. _____

    1. _____

    2. _____

B. _____

    1. _____

    2. _____

Conclusion: I think that _____ have more fun.

Step 4

Complete the response using your own outline from above.

I think that _____ have more fun than _____.
This is because _____.
For instance, _____
_____.
I think that _____.
For example, _____
_____.
For these reasons, I think that _____.

Integrated - Environment

Getting Ready to Write

A. Learn the words.

Key Vocabulary

barrier	anything that keeps one thing apart from another
rise	to move in an upward direction
power plant	a factory that makes electricity

TOEFL® Vocabulary

create	to make something
annually	every year
ton	a measurement of weight equal to 1000 kg
vehicle	a machine built for traveling in—like a car or truck
produce	to make something, usually in large amounts

Reading Passage

B. Read the first part of a passage. Then answer the questions.

> **Carbon Dioxide**
>
> Carbon dioxide is a gas. It is called CO_2. It creates a barrier. This traps heat around the Earth. This makes temperatures rise. This is known as global warming. CO_2 comes from two natural sources.
>
> First, it comes from active volcanoes.

1. What is the main idea of the passage?

   (A) Types of natural sources that produce CO_2

   (B) Process of how CO_2 pollutes the air

2. What do you think the rest of the passage and the lecture will talk about? Write two or three ideas below.

   _____

   _____

Practice

A. **Listen to the first part of a lecture. Then answer the question.** `Track 33`

What is the main idea of the lecture?

(A) Comparing natural CO_2 sources
(B) The problems with human-made CO_2

Note-taking

B. **Read the full passage. Then listen to the full lecture. Take notes in the boxes below.** `Track 34`

> ### Carbon Dioxide
>
> Carbon dioxide is a gas. It is called CO_2. It creates a barrier. This traps heat around the Earth. This makes temperatures rise. This is known as global warming. CO_2 comes from two natural sources.
>
> First, it comes from active volcanoes. As much as 255 million tons of CO_2 are put into the air annually by volcanoes. Air quality is poor in these areas. People living in these areas have health problems.
>
> Forest fires are another source. For example, forest fires in Indonesia in 1997 and 1998 released 23 billion tons of CO_2 into the air. That was almost half of all the CO_2 released into the air that year.

Reading

Main idea: CO_2 that causes global warming comes from _____
Key points:
 • Volcanoes put 255 million _____
 • Forest fires in Indonesia _____

Lecture

Main idea: Man-made CO_2 is _____
Key points:
 • Cars create a lot of _____
  - US drivers released 314 million tons of _____
 • Power plants _____
  - CO_2 from _____
  - Plants in the US give off 1.5 billion tons _____

Prompt

C. Read the prompt.

> Summarize the main points made in the lecture and explain how they challenge the main points in the reading passage.

Sample Response

D. Fill in the blanks of the sample response using phrases from the box. Use your notes to help you.

The reading explains how CO_2 is harmful. It explains that _____ that CO_2 is released into the air is through volcanoes and forest fires.

The lecture talks about how nature was not the _____. The lecture discusses how driving cars and using _____ releases much more carbon than nature does. The speaker says that US cars released 314 million tons of CO_2 into the air in 2004. The amount of CO_2 that humans make with cars and power plants is _____ than volcanoes and fires.

The lecture challenges the reading by showing how man-made CO_2 is worse than natural-made CO_2.

biggest problem	much more
two natural ways	power plants

TOEFL® Vocabulary Practice

E. Fill in the blanks with the correct words.

create	produces	annually	tons	vehicles

1. Florida _____ most of the orange juice for the US.
2. People in rural areas tend to drive bigger _____ than people in big cities.
3. A blue whale weights over 100 _____.
4. You can _____ many fun things with your hands using clay.
5. The American Super Bowl is held _____.

Test

Step 1

🎧 **Read the passage. Then listen to the lecture. Take notes in the boxes below.** Track 35

Methane Gas

Methane is a gas. It causes pollution. It is twenty times better at trapping heat than carbon dioxide. It is released into the air in many ways. Cows are a large part of the problem. They create a lot of methane gas. They do this in two ways.

First, due to the way cows digest food, they burp a lot. Methane gas in their stomachs passes through their mouths and into the air.

Second, cow waste also releases this gas. The waste also pollutes water sources when it washes downhill. Many think that cows are a serious threat to the environment.

Reading

Main idea: Cows create methane gas, which _____
Key points:
  • Cows _____
  • Cow waste releases gas and _____

Lecture

Main idea: Cows are not causing a lot _____
Key points:
  • Methane gas that cows produce can be _____
  • A natural chemical reduces the methane in their _____
  • Cow waste does not give off _____
  • Cow waste is _____

Step 2

🎧 **Read and listen to the prompt.** Track 36

Summarize the main points made in the lecture and explain how they challenge the main points in the reading passage.

Step 3

Complete the outline using your notes from Step 1.

Topic: The reading and the lecture discuss how cows release methane gas and cause pollution.
A. The reading says that
  1. cows create a lot of methane gas by _____
  2. water is polluted by _____
B. The lecture says that
  1. cows are not causing _____
  2. cow burping has already been reduced by 70% using a _____
  3. cow waste is natural and does not give off _____
Conclusion: The lecture challenges the reading by arguing that cows do not cause that much pollution.

Step 4

Complete the response using your outline from Step 3.

The reading and the lecture _____.
The reading says that cows create a lot of _____.
It also says that water is _____.
  In the lecture, the speaker challenges the reading by saying that cows are not
_____.
The speaker says that waste from cows' burping has already been reduced by ___
_____.
The speaker also says that cow waste is _____.
  The lecture challenges the reading by _____
_____.

Check-up

Fill in the blanks with the correct words.

adventure	mystery	giggle	barrier	power plants	rises

1. Some scientists like to study the _____ of UFOs.
2. Many young children _____ when they see clowns.
3. The sun _____ in the East and sets in the West.
4. Cowboys use a fence as a type of _____ to separate their cows.
5. Many people are worried about pollution caused by _____.
6. It is quite a(n) _____ to explore underground caves.

[09] Independent

Getting Ready to Write

A. Learn the words.

Key Vocabulary

bill	a document that shows money owed
borrow	to take and later give back
argue	to fight with words

TOEFL® Vocabulary

debt	a situation in which money is owed to others
anxiety	a worried, nervous feeling
owe	to have to pay money for something
steady	not changing
income	money received

B. Read the prompt. Then answer the questions.

Describe something you did recently that required you to pay money.

1. What was the activity?
   The activity was _____.

2. Why did you choose this activity?
   I chose this activity because _____.

3. Could you have done this activity without money?
   I could _____.

4. What is something else that you could have done without money?
   I could have _____.

Practice

A. Read the question.

Do you agree or disagree with the following statement?

People are happier when they have more money.

Use specific reasons and examples to support your answer.

Sample Response 1

B. Read the sample response. Then answer the question.

I think that people are happier when they have more money. First, you do not have to worry about paying your bills. People who do not have much money often have to borrow. Then they go into debt. Debt can cause anxiety. You cannot be happy if you are worried about how much you owe. Second, money means that you can buy what you need. My parents both have steady incomes. They are happy that they can buy what we need. They do not argue about not having money. People worry and argue less when they have enough money. This is why I believe people are happier when they have more money.

Which side of the statement does the response take?
(A) Agree   (B) Disagree

Outline

C. Complete the outline for the response.

Topic: People are _____ when they have more money.
A. You don't need to _____
   1. People who don't have money often _____
   2. Debt can cause _____
B. You can buy _____
   1. My mom and dad _____
   2. People _____
Conclusion: This is why I believe _____.

D. Underline the transitional words or phrases in the sample response.

E. Read the sample response. Then answer the question.

I don't think that people are happier if they have more money. Money alone cannot make someone truly happy. To begin, I think some people with big incomes are unhappy. My friend Paul's dad is rich. He is mean to Paul. Paul's family is not happy. My family is happy, but we don't have as much money. Also, I think money can make people worry. Some people want too much money. When they don't have it, it makes them unhappy. Paul's dad is like that. It makes his family argue. Therefore, people are happier when they don't want to have a lot of money. I am happy, but not because of money.

Which side of the statement does the response take?

(A) Agree   (B) Disagree

Outline

F. Complete the outline for the response.

Topic: I _____ people are happier if they have more money.
A. Some people with big incomes are _____
    1. Paul's dad is rich, but his family is _____
    2. My family is happy, but we _____
B. Money can make people _____
    1. Some people _____
    2. Paul's dad wants too much money, and it makes his _____
Conclusion: People are happier when _____.

G. Underline the transitional words or phrases in the sample response.

TOEFL® Vocabulary Practice

H. Fill in the blanks with the correct words.

debt	anxiety	owe	steady	income

1. Some people work second jobs to increase their _____.
2. Many people say that public speaking creates a lot of _____.
3. Most people want _____ jobs with good wages.
4. People who don't pay their credit card bills accumulate a lot of _____.
5. If someone takes out a loan at a bank, they _____ that bank money.

Test

Step 1

Read the question.

Do you agree or disagree with the following statement?

People are happier when they have more money.

Use specific reasons and examples to support your answer.

Step 2

State your opinion.

I _____ with the statement.

Step 3

Write an outline for your essay that will support your opinion.

Topic: I _____ when they have more money.
A. _____
    1. _____
    2. _____
B. _____
    1. _____
    2. _____
Conclusion: A person _____ be happy without money.

Step 4

Complete the response using your outline from above.

I _____ when they have more money.
First, I think _____.
For example, _____
_____.
Second, I think _____.
For instance, _____
_____.
I think a person _____ be happy without money.

Integrated - Health

Getting Ready to Write

A. Learn the words.

finally	in the end
level	a position above or below something
serving	an amount of food

TOEFL® Vocabulary

diagram	a drawing that explains something
government	the group that rules a country
section	a part of a larger thing
refer	to relate
category	a group of related things

Reading Passage

B. Read the first part of a passage. Then answer the questions.

> **The Food Pyramid**
>
> The food pyramid is a diagram. The US government made it in 1992. It is to teach people about healthy eating.
>
> At first, the government wanted to use the shape of a shopping cart. Then they tried a picture of a plate and bowl. They finally decided on the pyramid shape. It was the easiest to split into levels and sections. These separate sections refer to different food categories.

1. What is the main idea of the passage?

(A) Different food diagrams used by the US government

(B) A history and description of the food pyramid

2. What do you think the rest of the passage and the lecture will talk about? Write two or three ideas below.

_____

_____

Practice

Lecture

A. Listen to the first part of a lecture. Then answer the question. `Track 37`

What is the main idea of the lecture?

(A) Classifying the levels of the food pyramid.

(B) History of the food pyramid.

Note-taking

B. Read the full passage. Then listen to the full lecture. Take notes in the boxes below. `Track 38`

The Food Pyramid

The food pyramid is a diagram. The US government made it in 1992. It is to teach people about healthy eating.

At first, the government wanted to use the shape of a shopping cart. Then they tried a picture of a plate and bowl. They finally decided on the pyramid shape. It was the easiest to split into levels and sections. These separate sections refer to different food categories.

The largest level is at the bottom of the pyramid. This is the bread and grains group. The middle levels show fruit, vegetables, milk, and meat. At the top is the smallest section. This level is for fats and sweets.

Reading

Main idea: The food pyramid teaches people _____
Key points:
- The government decided on the _____
- The pyramid separates food categories into different _____

Lecture

Main idea: What each level of the _____
Key points:
- The large bottom of the pyramid means you should eat _____
- Only two to five servings of _____
- The top level of the pyramid shows _____

Prompt

C. Read the prompt.

Summarize the main points made in the lecture and explain how they support the main points in the reading passage.

Sample Response

D. Fill in the blanks of the sample response using phrases from the box. Use your notes to help you.

The reading explains what the food pyramid is and how it teaches people how to eat healthy. The pyramid suggests a _____ of foods to eat from different categories.

The lecture explains the categories in depth. The speaker says that the bottom group is for breads cereals, and pasta. People _____ a lot of these. The speaker also says that _____ contains sweets and fats. People should eat _____ food from this group.

certain amount	very little
the top group	should eat

TOEFL® Vocabulary Practice

E. Fill in the blanks with the correct words.

diagram	government	section	refer	category

1. Manhattan is one _____ of New York City.

2. Inventors will draw a _____ to help people understand their new products.

3. The _____ is in charge of making new laws.

4. Footnotes _____ to other parts of a book.

5. Geometry is a _____ of mathematics.

Test

Step 1

🎧 **Read the passage. Then listen to the lecture. Take notes in the boxes below.** `Track 39`

Changes to the Food Pyramid

The food pyramid was changed in 2004. The first diagram is gone. It was replaced with a different system. This happened for two reasons.

First, Americans were gaining weight. Some thought the old pyramid was part of the problem. The first level suggests eating many servings of bread and pasta.

Second, other research showed that different people need different amounts of food. The old pyramid suggested that all people eat the same amount. This is not true. Not all people need the same amount of food. These are the reasons that these new pyramids were made.

Reading

Main idea: The old food pyramid was replaced _____

Key points:
- Americans were _____
- The old pyramid was the _____
- Research showed that different people need _____

Lecture

Main idea: How the new system is _____

Key points:
- There are now twelve _____
- The food categories are now not divided by levels but are side _____
- The government has a _____
  - People can find their personal _____

Step 2

🎧 **Read and listen to the prompt.** `Track 40`

Summarize the main points made in the lecture and explain how they support the main points in the reading passage.

Step 3

Complete the outline using your notes from Step 1.

Topic: The reading and the lecture are about the new food pyramid.

A. The reading says that the new pyramids were developed because Americans were

_____

    1. They thought the old pyramid was _____

    2. People need different _____

B. The lecture says that there are now _____

    1. Each person can find his or her personal _____

    2. Food categories are now side by side and not _____

Conclusion: The lecture supports the reading because it gives examples of how the
           new pyramids are different from the old one.

Step 4

Complete the response using your outline from Step 3.

    The reading and the _____.
The reading says that the _____
_____.
The reading also says that research showed that different people need _____
_____.
    The lecture supports this by explaining that there are now _____
_____.
In the lecture, the speaker also says that the food categories are now _____
_____.
    The lecture supports the reading because _____
_____.

Check-up

Fill in the blanks with the correct words.

serving	argue	finally	bill	level	borrow

1. Credit card owners receive a _____ for their purchases each month.
2. Many banks allow people to _____ money to pay for college.
3. In 1969, the US _____ put a man on the moon after much research and testing.
4. Lawyers sometimes _____ in the courtroom when a trial is very difficult.
5. Most packages of food in the US provide the _____ size.
6. Some houses have one _____, while some have two or even three.

[10] Independent

Getting Ready to Write

A. Learn the words.

Key Vocabulary

celebrity	a famous person
gossip	to talk about others' private lives
role model	a person who is a good example to others

TOEFL® Vocabulary

personal	individual; private
devoted	caring very much about someone or something
affair	matters relating to personal life
trend	a new style
annoy	to pester; to irritate

B. Read the prompt. Then answer the questions.

Describe an experience when you copied something from a celebrity you saw on TV or in a magazine.

1. What was the experience?

It was _____.

2. Why did you do this?

I did this because _____.

3. How did you feel about this experience?

I felt _____.

4. What do you think of this idea?

I think that _____.

Practice

A. **Read the question.**

Do you agree or disagree with the following statement?

> People care too much about what celebrities do in their personal lives.

Use specific reasons and examples to support your answer.

Sample Response 1

B. **Read the sample response. Then answer the question.**

I think people care too much about what celebrities do in their personal lives. Celebrities are in the news all the time. There are some terrible things going on in the world. These things never make the news. News shows seem to think that everyone wants to see every small thing celebrities do. More important things should be on the news. Also, many TV shows are devoted to celebrity gossip. They are just people. But these shows talk about every tiny detail of their lives—their hairstyles, their vacations, their weight, etc. I don't care about any of this. However, I think others care too much.

Which side of the statement does the response take?
(A) Agree   (B) Disagree

Outline

C. **Complete the outline for the response.**

Topic: People _____ about what celebrities do.
A. Celebrities are in the news _____
    1. News does not show what is going on _____
    2. News seems to think everyone wants to _____
B. TV shows devoted to _____
    1. Celebrities are just _____
    2. TV shows talk about _____
Conclusion: I think others _____.

D. **Underline the transitional words or phrases in the sample response.**

E. Read the sample response. Then answer the question.

> I feel that we should care about what celebrities do in their personal lives. First, this is because young people look up to them. They can be good role models for us. For example, some celebrities do good things to help needy children. Others do things to help the environment. This sets a good example for all of us. If we did not care about their personal affairs, we would not see how they were helping the world. The second reason is that they start trends in our culture. Even if it annoys them, we need to know what they wear or where they eat or shop in their personal lives. This is how many popular trends start. New trends are important to kids like me.

Which side of the statement does the response take?

(A) Agree   (B) Disagree

Outline

F. Complete the outline for the response.

Topic: People _____ about what celebrities do.
A. They can be good _____
   1. They do things to help the _____
   2. They set good _____
B. They start _____
   1. We need to know what they wear, _____
   2. This is how popular trends that are _____
Conclusion: Knowing what celebrities do _____.

G. Underline the transitional words or phrases in the sample response.

TOEFL® Vocabulary Practice

H. Fill in the blanks with the correct words.

affairs	annoy	devoted	personal	trends

1. _____ thoughts are kept in a diary.

2. The Thanksgiving holiday is _____ to being thankful for what we have.

3. Many magazines reveal the _____ of famous people.

4. One of the latest _____ in communication is instant messaging.

5. Long lines _____ many people.

Test

Step 1

Read the question.

Do you agree or disagree with the following statement?

People care too much about what celebrities do in their personal lives.

Use specific reasons and examples to support your answer.

Step 2

State your opinion.

I _____ with the statement.

Step 3

Write an outline for your essay that will support your opinion.

Topic: People _____ about what celebrities do.
A. _____
    1. _____
    2. _____
B. _____
    1. _____
    2. _____
Conclusion: I think _____ what celebrities do.

Step 4

Complete the response using your outline from above.

I think that people _____ about what celebrities do.
This is because _____.
I think that because _____
_____.

I feel that _____.
For example, _____
_____.
For these reasons, I think _____ what celebrities do.

Integrated - Technology

Getting Ready to Write

A. Learn the words.

Key Vocabulary

tag	an attachment to an object
spy	to secretly find out information
chip	a very small electronic computer piece

TOEFL® Vocabulary

signal	information sent and received as electromagnetic waves through electronic equipment
device	a piece of equipment or machinery
track	to follow the location of something
shipment	the act of transporting goods
theft	the act of taking someone else's property without permission or payment

Reading Passage

B. Read the first part of a passage. Then answer the questions.

> **Spy Chips**
>
> There is a new technology being used today that helps businesses. It is called a radio frequency ID tag. These are also called spy chips. They are tiny chips put in many products. The chips act like radios. They give out a signal. Special devices track the chip. They can track it almost anywhere. These tags are helpful to businesses in two ways.

1. What is the main idea of the passage?

   (A) What a spy chip is

   (B) Comparing spy chips and radio frequency ID tags

2. What do you think the rest of the passage and the lecture will talk about? Write two or three ideas below.

   _____

   _____

Practice

Lecture

A. **Listen to the first part of a lecture. Then answer the question.** `Track 41`

What is the main idea of the lecture?

(A) Why people don't like spy chips

(B) Why stores don't like spy chips

Note-taking

B. **Read the full passage. Then listen to the full lecture. Take notes in the boxes below.** `Track 42`

Spy Chips

There is a new technology being used today that helps businesses. It is called a radio frequency ID tag. These are also called spy chips. They are tiny chips put in many products. The chips act like radios. They give out a signal. Special devices track the chip. They can track it almost anywhere. These tags are helpful to businesses in two ways.

First, they help store owners track new shipments. A store can find out if their next shipment is still at the factory or on a delivery truck.

Second, these tags help cut down on theft. For example, people who leave stores with stolen clothes can be tracked and caught. This is all because of the tiny chips sewn into the clothing.

Reading

Main idea: Radio frequency ID tags are helpful to _____
Key points:
- They are also called _____
- The tags help owners track new _____
- The tags help _____

Lecture

Main idea: People think spy chips are _____
Key points:
- Companies track _____
  - They get _____
- Chips could be a _____
  - They emit electromagnetic _____

C. Read the prompt.

Summarize the main points made in the lecture and explain how they challenge the main points in the reading passage.

Sample Response

D. Fill in the blanks of the sample response using phrases from the box. Use your notes to help you.

The reading explains how _____ tags help businesses. These chips are put into products and can be tracked almost anywhere.

The lecture argues that people do not think this is a good idea. The speaker talks about companies being able to track their customers. People think their _____ should be private. The speaker also says that the chips might be a _____. The tags emit _____ that might not be safe. People have stopped buying things with tags for these reasons.

personal information	radio frequency ID
health risk	electromagnetic energy

TOEFL® Vocabulary Practice

E. Fill in the blanks with the correct words.

device	signal	shipment	theft	track

1. It is against the law to commit _____.
2. Microchips are put into dolphins to _____ their movements.
3. The black box _____ on airplanes records the entire flight.
4. Ships used to use a telegraph to send a _____.
5. Grocery stores usually receive a _____ of fresh fruit and vegetables every day.

Test

Step 1

🎧 **Read the passage. Then listen to the lecture. Take notes in the boxes below.** `Track 43`

Tracking Devices

Parents can use technology to make sure their teens are safe. First, today's parents can have tracking devices placed in their kids' cell phones. These are tiny chips that give out a signal. They let a parent use a computer to find where their child is.

Another example is the car chip. These are similar to cell phone chips. They are used in the teen's car. These chips tell parents where kids are driving. They also tell parents how fast the teen is driving. For instance, parents will be told if their teen is driving too fast.

Reading

Main idea: Technology can help parents _____
Key points:
- Devices in cell phones tell parents _____
- Chips in cars tell parents where and _____

Lecture

Main idea: Technology does not really _____
Key points:
- Chips only track phones, not _____
- Chips in cars only give _____
  - They can't protect teens from _____

Step 2

🎧 **Read and listen to the prompt.** `Track 44`

Summarize the main points made in the lecture and explain how they challenge the main points in the reading passage.

Step 3

Complete the outline using your notes from Step 1.

Topic: The reading and the lecture discuss new technology parents can use.
A. The reading says that devices can be placed in a teenager's _____
    1. These devices _____
    2. The devices check where they are and how fast _____
B. The lecture states that the chip may not make _____
    1. The phone can be tracked but _____
    2. The chip cannot protect a teen from _____
Conclusion: The lecture challenges the reading, because it argues that the chips do
               not make teens any safer.

Step 4

Complete the sample response using your outline from Step 3.

    The reading and the lecture _____.
    The reading says that _____.
These devices help keep teens safe by _____
_____.
    However, the lecture states that the chip may not _____.
The speaker says that the phone can _____
_____.
    The lecture challenges the reading because _____
_____.

Check-up

Fill in the blanks with the correct words.

chip	spy	tag	celebrity	gossip	role models

1. Being a famous _____ means giving up a lot of privacy.
2. It would be an exciting job to be a _____.
3. Computers store memory on a tiny _____.
4. Teachers encourage students not to spread _____ at school.
5. Many products in malls these days have a _____ attached to them.
6. Parents need to work hard at being good _____ for their children.

Getting Ready to Write

A. Learn the words.

Key Vocabulary

peaceful	not violent
stab	to hurt someone with a sharp object
shoot	to hurt someone with a gun

TOEFL® Vocabulary

replicate	to copy
behave	to act in a certain way
criminal	someone who commits a crime
actually	really; in fact
award	to give something as a prize

B. Read the prompt. Then answer the questions.

Describe a video game you played or saw recently.

1. Describe whether the game was violent or not?
   The game was _____.

2. What did the game award points for?
   The game _____.

3. How do you think this game would make people feel?
   I think this game would _____.

4. In what ways was the game like real life?
   I think that this game was _____.

Practice

TOEFL® Question

A. Read the question.

Do you agree or disagree with the following statement?

Video games that have fighting or guns make people more violent.

Use specific reasons and examples to support your answer.

Sample Response 1

B. Read the sample response. Then answer the question.

I think that video games with guns do not make people more violent. First, video games are not real. They are just games. They do not replicate real life. My favorite video game has violence. However, just playing it does not mean I will behave this way. I know that killing is wrong. Second, not everyone that plays video games is violent. Only a few people are. I do not believe that this is because of video games. Criminals existed before video games. I play video games. I am not a criminal. I know right from wrong. Therefore, I do not think that video games make people violent.

Which side of the statement did the response take?
(A) Agree   (B) Disagree

Outline

C. Complete the outline for the response.

Topic: Video games with guns _____ people violent.
  A. Video games are _____
    1. Video games do not replicate _____
    2. It does not mean I will _____
  B. Not everyone that plays video games is _____
    1. Criminals existed _____
    2. I know right _____
Conclusion: I do not think that _____.

D. Underline the transitional words or phrases in the sample response.

E. Read the sample response. Then answer the question.

I think that video games make people more violent. First, I feel that people used to be more peaceful. Now, some people replicate crimes they see in video games. These games actually encourage people to act like criminals. I heard on the news about a twelve year old. He stabbed someone. Then he tried to steal a car. He was arrested. He said his video game gave him the idea. Second, the challenge in many video games is to hurt people. This teaches that it is good to hurt people. I played a game once that awarded points for shooting people. This is why I think these games teach people to behave violently.

Which side of the statement does the response take?

(A) Agree   (B) Disagree

Outline

F. Complete the outline for the response.

Topic: Video games _____ more violent.

A. People used to be _____

    1. Video games encourage _____

    2. A young boy stabbed someone and said _____

B. The challenge in many _____

    1. This teaches that it is _____

    2. Points are awarded for _____

Conclusion: These games teach people to _____.

G. Underline the transitional words or phrases in the sample response.

TOEFL® Vocabulary Practice

H. Fill in the blanks with the correct words.

replicate	criminal	actually	award	behave

1. Many people think that pollution is not _____ the cause of global warming.
2. The Olympic committee will _____ a gold medal for placing first in an event.
3. Parents teach their children to _____ well in public.
4. A _____ is sent to jail for committing a crime.
5. Some people think that children will _____ what their parents do.

Test

Step 1

Read the question.

Do you agree or disagree with the following statement?

Video games that have fighting or guns make people more violent.

Use specific reasons and examples to support your answer.

Step 2

State your opinion.

I _____ with the statement.

Step 3

Write an outline for your essay that will support your opinion.

Topic: I _____ video games that have fighting or guns make people more violent.

A. _____

   1. _____

   2. _____

B. _____

   1. _____

   2. _____

Conclusion: I think video games _____.

Step 4

Complete the response using your outline from above.

I _____ video games that have fighting or guns make people more violent.
To begin, I think video games _____.
Some video games _____
_____.
Second, _____.
I think this because _____
_____.
This is why I think video games _____
_____.

Integrated - Geography

Getting Ready to Write

A. Learn the words.

Key Vocabulary

sheet	a thin piece of something
fresh	clean
wear away	to destroy slowly; to erode

TOEFL® Vocabulary

glacier	a huge piece of ice made from compacted snow
differ	to have qualities that are not the same as something else
ecological	relating to the way living things live together
landscape	a part of the land seen from a particular place
fascinating	very interesting

Reading Passage

B. Read the first part of a passage. Then answer the questions.

Continental Glaciers

Continental glaciers are huge sheets of ice. They can be found in the coldest places on Earth. They differ from other glaciers in two ways.

First, they are very large. They are the biggest glaciers on the planet. They hold eighty percent of the Earth's fresh water.

1. What is the main idea of the passage?

(A) How continental glaciers form

(B) The characteristics of continental glaciers

2. What do you think the rest of the passage and the lecture will talk about? Write two or three ideas below.

_____

_____

Practice

Lecture

A. Listen to the first part of a lecture. Then answer the question. Track 45

What is the main idea of the lecture?

(A) The scale and power of continental glaciers

(B) Describing the world's largest glacier

Note-taking

B. Read the full passage. Then listen to the full lecture. Take notes in the boxes below. Track 46

Continental Glaciers

Continental glaciers are huge sheets of ice. They can be found in the coldest places on Earth. They differ from other glaciers in two ways.

First, they are very large. They are the biggest glaciers on the planet. They hold eighty percent of the Earth's fresh water. It would cause severe ecological changes if even a few melted.

Second, they have more power. They can change the landscape in bigger ways. Most glaciers wear away a little of the land around them. However, continental glaciers are very powerful. They can make valleys. They can also wear away mountain peaks.

Reading

Main idea: Continental glaciers are different from _____
Key points:
- Continental glaciers are very _____
- Continental glaciers can change the _____

Lecture

Main idea: The scale and power of continental _____
Key points:
- One sheet of ice covers _____
  - It is three meters _____
- If Antarctica glaciers melted, oceans would _____
- Over time, glaciers can change the _____

C. Read the prompt.

Summarize the main points made in the lecture and explain how they support the main points in the reading passage.

Sample Response

D. Fill in the blanks of the sample response using phrases from the box. Use your notes to help you.

The reading explains what a continental glacier is and the two ways that they differ from other glaciers. These glaciers are _____ and hold eighty percent of the planet's fresh water. They also have the power to _____ of the Earth by making valleys or wearing away mountain peaks.

The lecture explains the scale of these glaciers. The speaker says that a Greenland glacier is three kilometers thick _____. The speaker _____ that continental glacier bottoms wear away at the Earth. Over time, they can change what the Earth looks like.

very large	at some points
also points out	change the shape

TOEFL® Vocabulary Practice

E. Fill in the blanks with the correct words.

glacier	differ	ecological	landscape	fascinating

1. Extinction is one of the many current _____ concerns.
2. The discovery of DNA was _____ for scientists.
3. Antarctica is home to a very large _____.
4. A grape and a raisin _____ because a raisin is a dried grape.
5. Houses built in high places have a great view of the _____.

Test

Step 1

Read the passage. Then listen to the lecture. Take notes in the boxes below. **Track 47**

Glaciers

The Earth's glaciers are becoming smaller. Two ecological changes are causing this. To begin with, global warming is changing the Earth's climate. Even the coldest places on Earth are one degree warmer. The warmest days in the last five hundred years have all happened recently. This has caused lots of glaciers to melt.

However, there is another reason. The loss of forests near mountain glaciers also causes melting. Cutting down trees and plants mean less moisture is in the air. This makes the air dry. There are fewer clouds. This means less chance for rain or snow. Therefore, the glaciers start melting away.

Reading

Main idea: The glaciers on Earth are _____
Key points:
- Global warming is changing _____
- The loss of forests near mountain glaciers _____

Lecture

Main idea: Two of the world's glaciers are _____
Key points:
- The largest glacier in North America is _____
- The glacier on Mount Kilimanjaro is _____
  - Farmers have _____

Step 2

Read and listen to the prompt. **Track 48**

Summarize the main points made in the lecture and explain how they support the main points in the reading passage.

Step 3

Complete the outline using your notes from Step 1.

Topic: The reading and the lecture are about how the world's glaciers are disappearing.
A. The reading discusses two reasons for _____
    1. Global warming is _____
    2. The loss of forests near _____
B. The lecture gives examples of how this is affecting _____
    1. The largest glacier in North America is _____
    2. The loss of trees is making Mount Kilimanjaro's _____
       • Farmers have _____
Conclusion: The lecture supports the points made in the reading, because it gives examples of glaciers melting from global warming and the loss of trees.

Step 4

Complete the response using your outline from Step 3.

    The reading and the lecture are about _____.
The reading discusses _____.
One reason is because _____
and the other reason is _____.
    The lecture gives examples of _____.
The speaker talks about how the largest _____
_____.
The speaker also discusses how the loss of _____
_____.
    The lecture supports the points made in the reading, because _____
_____.

Check-up

Fill in the blanks with the correct words.

sheet	fresh	wear away	shoot	stab	peaceful

1. Activists look for a _____ way to end conflicts.

2. Water that flows fast will begin to _____ the walls of a river.

3. Grocery stores sell _____ fruit and throw the old fruit away.

4. A fork helps us eat because its sharp points let us _____ our food to pick it up.

5. Many people learn how to _____ a gun in the army.

6. When rivers freeze in the winter, the top becomes a solid _____ of ice.

[12] Independent

Getting Ready to Write

A. Learn the words.

Key Vocabulary

language	a spoken or written form of communication
bilingual	able to speak two languages well
translate	to put into another language

TOEFL® Vocabulary

foreign	of another country
require	to need
scarce	very few
asset	a useful or good thing
native	from a particular place

B. Read the prompt. Then answer the questions.

Describe someone you know who speaks another language.

1. Who is this person?
This person is _____.

2. Why do they speak another language?
He/she does because _____.

3. What are some benefits of speaking another language?
Some benefits of speaking another language are _____
_____.

4. Why would someone like to learn to speak another language?
Someone might want to learn to speak another language because _____
_____.

Practice

A. Read the question.

Do you agree or disagree with the following statement?

All students should learn a foreign language in school.

Use specific reasons and examples to support your answer.

Sample Response 1

B. Read the sample response. Then answer the question.

I think that all students should learn a foreign language in school. There are two benefits to this. First, learning a foreign language can help you get into college. Most colleges require that you have studied a foreign language. Some only accept students who have taken at least two years of courses. A second benefit is more options for jobs. You can apply for higher paying jobs. In many cities, bilingual people are scarce. Many businesses consider bilingual people an asset. Therefore, people who can translate often make good incomes. This is why I believe that it is good to learn another language.

Which side of the statement does the response take?

(A) Agree   (B) Disagree

Outline

C. Complete the outline for the response.

Topic: Students _____ learn a foreign language in school.
A. Helps get into _____
    1. Most colleges require students to have _____
    2. Some only _____
B. Helps get a higher paying _____
    1. Businesses think bilingual people are an _____
    2. People who _____
Conclusion: I believe _____.

D. Underline the transitional words or phrases in the sample response.

E. Read the sample response. Then answer the question.

I do not think that all students should learn a foreign language. I feel this way for two reasons. First of all, I think that students already have too much to learn. They have to learn many subjects, and time is scarce. These subjects take up a lot of time. To add a different language would be difficult. The second reason is that students have already learned their native language. They live in a country that speaks that language. If they do not plan on traveling a lot, they do not need to know another language. They already have what they need to talk and work with people where they live. I think students should spend time learning other things.

Which side of the statement does the response take?

(A) Agree

(B) Disagree

Outline

F. Complete the outline for the response.

Topic: I _____ that all students should learn a foreign language in school.
A. Students already have too much _____
   1. They have many subjects and _____
   2. A different _____
B. Students already learned their _____
   1. They live in a country that _____
   2. They already have what they need to _____
Conclusion: I think _____.

G. Underline the transitional words or phrases in the sample response.

TOEFL® Vocabulary Practice

H. Fill in the blanks with the correct words.

asset	foreign	native	requires	scarce

1. People from _____ countries often find it difficult to talk to people in a new country.

2. Training for a marathon _____ many hours of practice.

3. Water is _____ in desert areas.

4. Good speaking skills are a(n) _____ in many jobs.

5. Brown bears are _____ to Alaska.

Test

Step 1

Read the question.

Do you agree or disagree with the following statement?

All students should learn a foreign language in school.

Use specific reasons and examples to support your answer.

Step 2

State your opinion.

I _____ with the statement.

Step 3

Write an outline for your essay that will support your opinion.

Topic: I think students _____ learn a foreign language in school.
A: _____
    1. _____
    2. _____
B. _____
    1. _____
    2. _____
Conclusion: I _____ to learn another language in school.

Step 4

Complete the response using your outline from above.

    I think students _____ learn a foreign language in school.
This is because _____.
For example, _____
_____.
I think that _____
_____.
For these reasons, I _____.

Integrated - Music

Getting Ready to Write

A. Learn the words.

Key Vocabulary

mix	a combination
massive	very large (sometimes shortened to mass)
hit	something that is very popular

TOEFL® Vocabulary

phenomenon	an unusual and impressive happening
audience	the group of people that a production is for
appeal	to be of interest
perform	to share a skill such as acting or singing in front of an audience
icon	a symbol

Reading Passage

B. Read the first part of a passage. Then answer the questions.

> #### Rock 'n' Roll
>
> Rock 'n' Roll music is truly a phenomenon. It is a mix of many types of music. This genre started in the mid-1950s. Many feel Rock 'n' Roll began with Elvis Presley. A famous magazine said that Elvis introduced Rock 'n' Roll in 1954. This is when his first record was released.

1. What is the main idea of the passage?

(A) Beginnings of the Rock 'n' Roll genre

(B) Types of Rock 'n' Roll musician

2. What do you think the rest of the passage and the lecture will talk about? Write two or three ideas below.

_____

_____

Practice

A. Listen to the first part of a lecture. Then answer the question. Track 49

What is the main idea of the lecture?

(A) How Rock 'n' Roll began

(B) Comparing Rock 'n' Roll artists

Note-taking

B. Read the full passage. Then listen to the full lecture. Take notes in the boxes below. Track 50

Rock 'n' Roll

Rock 'n' Roll music is truly a phenomenon. It is a mix of many types of music. This genre started in the mid-1950s. Many feel Rock 'n' Roll began with Elvis Presley. A famous magazine said that Elvis introduced Rock 'n' Roll in 1954. This is when his first record was released.

Another reason many say Elvis started Rock 'n' Roll is his audiences. This was the first time music had a mass appeal across America. He performed in front of thousands of teen fans. They were screaming and crying. He is known as the king of Rock 'n' Roll. He is an icon in the world of music.

Reading

Main idea: Elvis started _____

Key points:
- A famous magazine said Elvis _____
- This was the first time music had _____
  - Elvis performed in front _____

Lecture

Main idea: Elvis didn't truly start _____

Key points:
- One of most popular hits was recorded before _____
  - *Rock Around the Clock* by Bill Haley and _____
- Radio DJ called Alan Freed came up with the _____
  - He also produced the first _____

C. Read the prompt.

> Summarize the main points made in the lecture and explain how they challenge the main points in the reading passage.

Sample Response

D. Fill in the blanks of the sample response using phrases from the box. Use your notes to help you.

The reading explains the beginnings of Rock 'n' Roll. Many believe that Elvis Presley introduced Rock 'n' Roll. This is because he had a _____ and performed in front of thousands of fans.

The lecture claims that Rock 'n' Roll did not begin with Elvis. The speaker credits _____ with the first Rock 'n' Roll hit. The song was called *Rock Around the Clock*. This song was recorded before Elvis's first record. The lecture also states that _____, a radio DJ, introduced Rock 'n' Roll to audiences in 1951. This was _____ Elvis produced his first record.

> Alan Freed   three years before
> Bill Haley and the Comets   mass appeal

TOEFL® Vocabulary Practice

E. Fill in the blanks with the correct words.

appeal	audience	icon	perform	phenomenon

1. The Aurora Borealis, or Northern Lights, are a natural _____.
2. The _____ always appreciates it when performers give a great show.
3. The Harry Potter books _____ to all ages.
4. Actors dream of being asked to _____ on Broadway.
5. President Abraham Lincoln is a(n) _____ of the Civil War era.

Test

Step 1

Read the passage. Then listen to the lecture. Take notes in the boxes below. `Track 51`

> ### Rock 'n' Roll
>
> Rock 'n' Roll has a mix of many different types of music. However, most agree that the strongest ties are to African-American blues music.
>
> First, Rock 'n' Roll used the same kind of instruments as the new blues. This was electric guitars and drums. It became known as rhythm and blues. Or "R and B" for short. It started in the 1940s.
>
> Second, R and B artists became icons. Little Richard and Chuck Berry were two of the first. They set the stage for future artists. Artists such as Bill Haley and Elvis Presley. They also prepared audiences for what was coming next—Rock 'n' Roll.

Reading

Main idea: Rock 'n' Roll music has _____
Key points:
- Used the same _____
- R and B artists became _____
  - Little Richard and Chuck Berry prepared audiences _____

Lecture

Main idea: Rock 'n' Roll really came from _____
Key points:
- Rockabilly music is _____
- Rockabilly musicians were _____
  - Wanda Jackson was _____

Step 2

Read and listen to the prompt. `Track 52`

Summarize the main points made in the lecture and explain how they challenge the main points in the reading passage.

Step 3

Complete the outline using your notes from Step 1.

Topic: The reading and the lecture are about where Rock 'n' Roll came from.

A. The reading says that
  1. Rock 'n' Roll has strong ties _____
  2. R and B artists prepared _____
     • Little _____
     • Chuck _____
B. The lecture explains that Rock 'n' Roll _____
  1. Like country music _____
  2. Rockabilly artists, like Wanda Jackson, were _____

Conclusion: The lecture challenges the reading by saying Rock 'n' Roll music came
from rockabilly music, not the blues.

Step 4

Complete the response using your outline from Step 3.

The reading and the lecture _____.
The reading says that Rock 'n' Roll has _____.
The reading also says that R and B _____
_____.
The lecture explains that Rock 'n' Roll _____.
The speaker says that rockabilly music was _____.
The speaker also talks about _____.
The lecture challenges the reading _____
_____.

Check-up

Fill in the blanks with the correct words.

| language | hits | massive | bilingual | translate | mix |

1. The sun is _____ compared to the Earth.

2. Many Hispanic Americans are _____, speaking both English and Spanish.

3. A labra-doodle is a _____ of a Labrador Retriever and a Poodle.

4. The Beatles had many number one _____ in the 1960s.

5. Subtitles in movies _____ what is being said in another language.

6. Learning to speak another _____ is good exercise for the brain.

[Review 2]

Step 1

Read the question.

Do you agree or disagree with the following statement?

> Money can buy happiness.

Use specific reasons and examples to support your answer.

Step 2

State your opinion.

I _____ with the statement.

Step 3

Write an outline for your essay that will support your opinion.

Topic: Money _____ buy happiness.
A. _____
    1. _____
    2. _____
B. _____
    1. _____
    2. _____
Conclusion: For these reasons, I _____.

Step 4

Complete the response using your outline from above.

I think that money _____ buy happiness.
I think this because _____.
For example, _____
_____.
In addition, _____.
For instance, _____
_____.
It is for these reasons that I _____.

Step 1

🎧 Read the passage. Then listen to the lecture. Take notes in the boxes below. **Track 53**

> ### The ATM
>
> The ATM has changed our lives and, in particular, made it easier to spend money. Before it, you had to go to the bank to get money. Often, the bank would be closed. If you needed money, you would have to wait. You might have to wait all weekend. That could often cause a crisis. But now you can get money anytime, anywhere. Even if you are in a foreign country. Just go to the ATM.
>
> In fact, spending money keeps getting easier. More and more people now pay with credit cards and there are even other technologies coming to help us pay for items. Soon, we won't even have to bother going to the ATM. If the trend continues, we won't need cash at all.

Reading

Main idea: The ATM made it easier _____
Key points:
  • Before ATMs, we had to go to the _____
  • ATMs made it easy to get money _____
  • People now pay with _____
  • Soon, we won't need _____

Lecture

Main idea: Technology has changed how we _____
Key points:
  • Not many people carry cash _____
  • We may not need to take cash out or use _____
  • Some countries use _____

Step 2

🎧 Read and listen to the prompt. **Track 54**

Summarize the main points made in the lecture and explain how they support the main points in the reading passage.

Step 3

Complete the outline using your notes from step 1.

Topic: The reading and the lecture talk about how technologies have changed how we
use money.

A. The reading talks about

    1. how ATMs made spending _____

      • Before ATMs, you had to _____

    2. how we might _____

B. The lecture says

    1. very few people carry a lot of _____

    2. we may not need cash or _____

      • Some countries already use _____

      • It will be very easy to _____

Conclusion: The lecture supports the passage by giving an example of how ATMs are
useful and how we might not need cash in the future.

Step 4

Complete the response using your outline from Step 3.

> The reading and the lecture talk about how _____
> _____.
> The reading talks about _____.
> Before ATMs, you _____.
> The author went on to say that, we _____.
>   The lecture supports this by talking about how very few people _____
> _____.
> The speaker discusses how we may not _____.
> Some countries already _____.
> _____.
>   The lecture supports the passage by _____
> _____.

Step 1

🎧 Read the passage. Then listen to a lecture. Take notes in the boxes below. `Track 55`

The Charts

The charts are a tool in the music industry. They show the popularity of the latest songs. New songs are ranked, with number one being the most popular. Any genre of music can be featured on the charts. But, most of it falls in the pop music category.

Some pop icons always appear on the charts. Madonna would be an example. If she releases a song, it will be on the charts. This is because audiences are used to her music. They like it. They know what to expect. Music awards are also based, in part, on these charts.

Reading

Main idea: The charts show the popularity of _____
Key points:
- New songs are _____
- Any genre of music can be featured but _____
- Certain pop icons _____

Lecture

Main idea: People should not just listen to _____
Key points:
- Only pop music is _____
- If the artist is not famous or doesn't have a lot of money, then they won't

_____

- The charts make it difficult for unknown _____

Step 2

🎧 Read and listen to the prompt. `Track 56`

Summarize the main points made in the lecture and explain how they differ from the main points in the reading passage.

Step 3

Complete the outline using your notes from Step 1.

    Topic: The reading and the lecture are about music charts.

    A. The reading says the charts are a tool to show _____

        1. Most music on the charts is _____

        2. Other genres might be _____

    B. The lecture says that people _____

        1. If the artist is not famous or rich, _____

        2. The charts make it difficult _____

    Conclusion: They differ mainly because the lecture talks about how the charts make it difficult for other types of music and artists to be heard.

Step 4

Complete the response using your outline from Step 3.

    The reading and the lecture are about _____.

They are a tool the music industry uses to _____.

It goes on to explain that most music _____.

However, other genres might be _____.

    The lecture says that _____.

This is bad because _____.

The speaker goes on to say that, _____.

    The reading and the lecture differ _____

_____.

Step 1

Read the question.

Do you agree or disagree with the following statement?

It is better to go to a big school than a small school.

Use specific reasons and examples to support your answer.

Step 2

State your opinion.

I _____ with the statement.

Step 3

Write an outline for you essay that will support your opinion.

Topic: The best size school to go to is _____.
A. _____
    1. _____
    2. _____
B. _____
    1. _____
    2. _____
Conclusion: I think _____.

Step 4

Complete the response using your outline from above.

I think the best size school to go to is _____.
I think this because _____.
For example, _____
_____.
Furthermore, _____.
I think this because _____
_____.
In conclusion, I think _____
_____.

Writing 1
Worksheets

Unit 1 Worksheet: Simple Sentences

A simple sentence is also known as an independent clause. It contains a subject and a verb. It gives all the information needed to express one independent thought. It is very important to understand simple sentences as every other sentence structure builds upon it.

Examples
Bob goes to middle school.
Julie ran.
We drove to dance class yesterday.
I study every day for my science class.

A. Put a check (✓) beside the complete sentences and a cross (✗) beside the incomplete sentences.

1. Families offer lots of support. _____
2. I for a youth Olympic soccer team. _____
3. Kids need loving families. _____
4. Today, many families near each other. _____
5. Severe competition in the world today. _____
6. They had faith in me. _____
7. Family members give lots of guidance. _____
8. Had a firm rule about eating dinner together. _____

B. Fill in the blanks with the most appropriate words.

adopted	legal	vote	future
permitted	tax	afford	seemingly

1. New laws were _____ to limit African Americans' freedom.
2. It was not _____ for African Americans to use the same restrooms as whites.
3. The court's decisions _____ unfair treatment.
4. People _____ for new leaders in this country.
5. People had to pay a _____ to the government in order to vote.
6. It was a _____ small cost.
7. Many people could not _____ to pay it.
8. Slaves hoped for a better _____.

C. Use the following subjects and verbs to write your own simple sentences.

Subjects:	I	Dad	They	We	Mark
Verbs:	permit	visit	swim	offer	like

1. _____
2. _____
3. _____
4. _____
5. _____

Unit 2 Worksheet: Subject-Verb Agreement

Subjects and verbs must agree with each other in number. The verb form can change depending on whether the subject is singular or plural. If a subject is singular, its verb must also be singular. If a subject is plural, its verb must also be plural.

Examples

The girl plays.   The girls play.

The woman trains seals.   The women train seals.

A. Put a check (✓) beside the sentences with correct agreement and a cross (X) beside the incorrect sentences.

1. They also knows your flaws. _____
2. He lets me build my math problems. _____
3. The secretary answers the phone. _____
4. Her parents is lawyers. _____
5. My relatives usually visit at Thanksgiving. _____
6. My dad drives a tractor. _____
7. The teacher hardly know you at all. _____
8. She multiplies big numbers easily. _____
9. Students studies hard for their exams. _____
10. I feels parents are great teachers. _____

B. Circle the correct verb form to complete each sentence.

1. Picasso **was/were** a famous cubist painter.
2. Many people **like/likes** his style.
3. The people in his paintings **look/looks** poor.
4. She **seem/seems** sad.
5. Picasso's art **imitate/imitates** things he saw in his daily life.
6. His work **show/shows** a different side of humanity.
7. The second reason **is/are** that his art did not look real.
8. Many art fans today **appreciate/appreciates** his unusual style.
9. Artists **find/finds** different beauty in common things.
10. A modern artist **use/uses** squares and triangles for people's shapes.

C. Change the nouns and verbs in these sentences from singular to plural.

1. The town is very large.

   _____

2. The dog takes a nap every afternoon.

   _____

3. The shirt looks like it's from a different era.

   _____

Unit 3 Worksheet: Transition Words—Conjunctive Adverbs

Transition words link related sentences. Conjunctive adverbs are one kind of transition word. Some common conjunctive adverbs include *also*, *however*, and *therefore*. Each one denotes a specific kind of transition or relationship between two sentences. *Also* indicates addition. *However* indicates contrast. *Therefore* indicates effect from a logical cause. Conjunctive adverbs can be placed at several positions within a sentence.

Examples
Video games are not enjoyable. **Also**, they are too expensive.
Stanley is reading a magazine. Raj is **also** reading a magazine.
Drake is not trendy. Garth, **however**, is always aware of the most popular brands.
She did well on the test; **however**, she was not satisfied with the results.
This restaurant is very popular. **Therefore**, it is necessary to make a reservation.
Anna's brothers used to tease her about her hair. She is **therefore** always conscious of her appearance.

A. Complete the sentences with *also, however,* or *therefore.*

1. Her high-heel shoes hurt her feet. _____, she wears them all the time.
2. They have sharp claws to grasp their prey. They _____ have sharp teeth to chew through tough skin and bones.
3. They have a hard time digesting plants. _____, they only digest a little of what they eat.
4. A plant-eating animal's digestive tract is twenty-seven times longer than its body. _____, a tiger's digestive tract is only five times the length of its body.
5. A panda's short digestive tract is made for meat. _____, a panda doesn't digest bamboo well.
6. African Americans were free. _____, they were still not treated the same as others.

B. Match these sentences to the sentences that logically follow below.

1. My friend is always self-conscious about her outward appearance and wastes a lot of money on beauty magazines. _____
2. Their sharp teeth helped them take the hard coverings off thick plants. _____
3. Pandas use their strong jaws to crush bamboo stems. _____
4. Picasso painted poor people on the streets. _____
5. The areas for whites and African Americans were supposed to be equal. _____
6. There was not enough prey in the area to feed all the carnivores. _____

(A) However, they had a hard time digesting plants.
(B) Some animals, therefore, had to use their carnivore traits to eat plants.
(C) Also, he painted sad people in jail.
(D) Therefore, I think people are happier when they do not worry so much about fashion.
(E) The areas for whites, however, were much nicer.
(F) They also use their teeth to pull off the outward part of the plant.

C. Use the prompts to write two sentences connected by a conjunctive adverb.

1. _____

   Write about a trait you find attractive, but your friend does not. (however)

2. _____

   Write about two different types of material that you enjoy reading. (also)

3. _____

   Write about the last time someone made you angry and the result. (therefore)

Unit 4 Worksheet: Modals (*Should & Must*)

Modals are verbs that modify the meaning or mood of another verb. There are certain grammar rules that apply to modals. First, modals do not conjugate; they keep the same form for all subjects. Second, modals are placed between the subject and the main verb in indicative sentences. Third, in interrogative questions, the modal and subject reverse position. Therefore, the modal comes first, then the subject, then the main verb.

Should is a modal that is most commonly used to give advice. It can also be used to express obligation or expectation. *Must* is another modal. It can be used to show certainty or obligation.

Examples
People with high cholesterol **should** exercise regularly. (advice)
I **should** be at work by 8:30 every day. (obligation)
Kelly **should** be here in a few minutes. (expectation)
You **must** hand in assignments on time. (obligation)
You have been sneezing all day; you **must** be getting sick. (certainty)

A. Write the function of the modal used in the sentence (advice, obligation, expectation, or certainty).

1. For this job, you **must** be able to speak well on the phone. _____
2. Students **should** listen to their teachers. _____
3. Hal **should** be here for his interview at four o'clock. _____
4. Jenn's computer is turned off. She **must** have gone home already. _____
5. Children **must** learn how to multiply before they learn how to divide. _____
6. To make a good impression, you **should** speak clearly at the interview. _____
7. You **must** hold the prism up to a light source in order to see the color spectrum. _____
8. The woman experimenting with the prism **must** be the science teacher. _____

B. Read the sentence. Then unscramble the response.

1. I'm really hungry. _____
   I / order / Should / spaghetti? / pizza / or
2. A: John wants to see a spectrum. B: _____
   prism. / get / He / a / should
3. A: I have an exam now, and I didn't study! B: _____
   nervous. / be / You / must
4. A: I really want to get this job. B: _____
   during / not / the / You / must / interview. / mumble
5. A: I want to plant a lot of flowers over there. B: _____
   these / should / You / seeds. / scatter
6. Look at those dark clouds. _____
   It / raining / soon. / start / should

Unit 5 Worksheet: Confusing Verbs and Nouns

Nouns are words that represent things or ideas. Verbs are words that represent actions or states. Sometimes, a noun and a verb can have the same spelling. Sometimes, the different noun forms and verb forms of the same root word can be confusing.

Noun	Verb	Noun	Verb
help	help	advice	advise
look	look	consideration	consider
address	address	decision	decide
benefit	benefit	destruction	destroy
profit	profit	production	produce
contract	contract		
cost	cost		

A. Label the words in bold either nouns (N) or verbs (V).

1. I really need your **help** to download this software. _____
2. These computers **cost** a lot of money. _____
3. Time wasted on deleting spam reduces a company's **profit**. _____
4. Computers **help** us communicate through email every day. _____
5. Computers can **benefit** students by making it easier to find information for their homework. _____
6. The **look** on my sister's face before the big test told me she was feeling a lot of stress. _____
7. Owners can usually start making a **profit** right away. _____
8. You can reach me at this email **address** at any time. _____

B. Complete the sentences with the correct form of words from the box.

> decide/decision   produce/production   advise/advice   consider/consideration

1. Franchise owners can benefit from the _____ of other owners.
2. Being part of a group of companies selling the same product can reduce the cost of _____.
3. The hard part is trying to _____ which franchise to use.
4. Before investing, it is important to _____ the pros and cons of both types of franchise.
5. Her business partner _____ her not to sign the contract.
6. My uncle owns a business that _____ customized mouse pads.
7. After much _____, we have decided that Earl is the best employee to deal with this problem.
8. Important _____ can cause a lot of stress in a person's life.

C. Rewrite the sentences, using the noun form of the verb in bold.

1. My teacher really **helped** me understand math better.

   _____

2. My parents **advised** me to major in English literature at university.

   _____

3. That sports car **costs** too much money for my budget.

   _____

Unit 6 Worksheet: Simple Present and Verbs for Citing

The simple present tense is used for repeated, habitual actions, or constant states.
Example: John **wakes up** at 7:00 every morning. He **lives** in an apartment.

The simple present tense is also used when citing details from a text or an other academic source. These texts can be considered to be in a constant state.
Example: The research in the latest UN paper **indicates** that disease rates are decreasing.

When citing for academic purposes, it is better to avoid repetition of the same citation word, especially *say*. Different citation words have different meanings or levels of emphasis.

Neutral	For Emphasis	For Contradiction
comment explain note indicate observe remark point out state suggest claim	emphasize maintain assert argue contend	deny refute challenge

A. Circle the correct form of the citation verb to complete each sentence.

1. The reading **explain/explains** how fission theory was the first to explain how the moon was formed.
2. The speaker **note/notes** that the rocks from the Earth's orbit and the rocks on the moon are made of different chemicals.
3. The text **state/states** that people used to believe the theory that the moon's craters were caused by volcanoes.
4. The writers **claim/claims** that principals have more experience in grading than students do.
5. The lecturer also **emphasize/emphasizes** that Jim Crow laws unfairly separated African Americans from other peoples.
6. The speaker **challenge/challenges** the reading by noting different reasons leading to the start of the blue period.

B. Rewrite the sentences, changing the citing verbs used to one from the list above.

1. The writer **says** that student evaluations would allow teachers to know how much they are appreciated.

   _____

2. The lecturer **says** that Dr. Johnson's research is incorrect, and **says** that her own research resulted in the only correct data.

   _____

Unit 7 Worksheet: *Will* for prediction

One of the most common ways to talk about the future is with *will*. There are three main ways to use *will* to talk about the future. *Will* is used when there is no prior plan or decision to do something and when the decision is made at the time of speaking. In this context, it is often used with the verb *think*. *Will* is also often used to make a prediction. *Will* is also used with *be* when a firm plan has been made and is not spontaneous. The negative form is *will not* or *won't*.

Examples
I think I'll have the steak, please. (immediate decision)
The sun is shining, so I think I'll walk to school today. (immediate decision)
Billy **won't** be frightened if you turn on his night light. (prediction)
She **will** be a best-selling author someday. (prediction)
There **will** be a prize for the best costume. (planned action)
The counselor **will** see you at three o'clock. (planned action)

A. Indicate the function of *will* in the following sentences. Write Id if it is used for an immediate decision, Pr for prediction, or Pa for a planned action.

1. It will make them feel better to express their emotions. _____
2. I won't be at school tomorrow morning. I have a doctor's appointment. _____
3. The kids will see that it's all right to feel sad sometimes. _____
4. It looks cold outside. I think I'll wear this green sweater. _____
5. A person who reads about history will probably become quite wise. _____
6. Grandma will come to our house for Thanksgiving. Mom invited her last week. _____

B. Match the sentences that follow logically.

1. This autobiography is really interesting. _____
2. Will you go meet that author signing books at the library? _____
3. When I have kids, I want them to admire me. _____
4. Molly reads books from many different genres. _____
5. It just started raining. _____
6. Will you meet Anna this weekend? _____

    (A) Yes. We'll go to a movie Saturday night.
    (B) I'll lend you my umbrella.
    (C) Yes. I will go with Mark.
    (D) Yeah? I think I'll read it, too.
    (E) She'll be a very wise woman someday.
    (F) I'm sure they will.

C. Answer the questions with a sentence using *will*.

1. What plans do you have for this weekend?

    _____

2. What do you think the weather will be like tomorrow?

    _____

Unit 8 Worksheet: Verb + Noun Phrases (*Have, Make, & Take*)

Some verb + noun combinations have fixed meanings that are easily confused by students. Students must memorize the combinations and their meanings. Remember that the verb still must be put into the correct tense and conjugation, while the noun remains the same.

make +	a mistake	a profit	progress	a decision		
have +	lunch	dinner	a headache	fun	a cold	
take +	a break	a risk	care	notes	time	action

A. Choose the best noun to complete the sentences.

1. Young people have more _____ than old people. (progress / fun)
2. They use tried-and-true methods to avoid making costly _____. (mistakes / headaches)
3. Owners can usually start making _____ right away. (notes / profits)
4. The detectives didn't take _____ until they had solved the mystery. (a cold / a break)
5. There is an abundant amount of restaurants where we can have _____. Just choose one. (dinner / a profit)
6. Did you take _____ in yesterday's science class? I wasn't there. (notes / a mistake)

B. Complete the sentences with a logical verb + noun collocation from the list above.

1. Laurie likes to _____. She always looks for adventure.
2. My grandmother _____ more _____ than a lot of my friends. She always tells jokes and makes people laugh.
3. Reducing the amount of CO_2 gas released by our cars would help us _____ in slowing global warming.
4. It will _____ for governments to create alternative sources of energy to the coal-burning power plants that are in widespread use today. It won't happen quickly.
5. Jim was stuck in traffic for two hours. Now, he _____ and needs some medicine.
6. The government recently _____ to force car makers to produce vehicles that release less CO_2 into the atmosphere.

C. Answer the questions in a full sentence.

1. If you could have dinner with anyone in the world, who would it be? Why?
   _____
2. Have you ever made an embarrassing mistake? What happened?
   _____
3. What was the biggest risk you ever took?
   _____

Unit 9 Worksheet: Compound Sentences

Compound sentences include two independent clauses joined by a coordinating conjunction. Four major coordinating conjunctions are *and*, *but*, *so*, and *or*. *And* is used to indicate addition. *But* is used to indicate contrast. *So* is used to indicate cause and effect. *Or* is used to show choice. In compound sentences, a comma is placed after the first independent clause and before the coordinating conjunction. Coordinating conjunctions can also be used to connect grammatically equal parts of a sentence in non-compound sentences. In this case, a comma is not used before the conjunction.

Examples
They go into debt, **and** debt can cause anxiety.
My friend Paul's dad is rich, **but** Paul's family is not happy.
My parents have enough money to buy what they need, **so** they do not argue about money.
We can use the old food pyramid, **or** we can make a new one.

A. **Put a check (✓) beside the compound sentences and a cross (✗) next to those that are not.**

   1. The biggest level of the food pyramid is the bread and grains group. _____
   2. Americans gained weight after the first food pyramid was created, so the government made a new one. _____
   3. People should eat six to eleven servings of bread and pasta, but only two to five servings of fruits and vegetables. _____
   4. Two to three servings of milk or cheese should be eaten each day. _____
   5. She thinks they look good, so she wears them. _____
   6. Rich people do not have to worry about paying their bills, so they are happier than poor people. _____

B. **Complete the sentences with *and, but, so,* or *or.***

   1. It's OK to eat lots of oatmeal, _____ don't eat lots of oatmeal cookies.
   2. They use tried-and-true business ideas, _____ a new owner will not have to make costly mistakes.
   3. We can borrow money to buy a car now, _____ save our money to buy a car later.
   4. The food pyramid is a diagram, _____ it is split into different levels and sections.
   5. I don't have a lot of money, _____ I am happy.
   6. My mom has a steady income, _____ she doesn't have to worry about bills and debt.

C. **Answer the questions with compound sentences.**

   1. What two things will you do next weekend?

   _____

   2. What food do you like to eat, but your parents do not?

   _____

   3. Why are you studying English?

   _____

Unit 10 Worksheet: Transitions for Presenting Supporting Points

When writing an essay, you should present several points to support your argument. Transitional sequence words can be used to organize those points in a logical order. Many of these words are similar to words used to sequence for time; however, in this case, they represent logical order.

Sequence	Addition
First, To begin, In the first place, To start	Furthermore
Second, Secondly, Next	Plus
Third, Thirdly, Next	Moreover
In the end, Finally, Last, Lastly	Again
	In addition

A. Choose the best transition to complete the sentences.

1. First, young people look up to celebrities. **To start,** / **Second,** celebrities start trends in our culture.

2. There are several reasons you shouldn't ask coworkers personal questions. **In the first place,** / **Moreover,** they might worry about you spreading gossip about their private information.

3. Secondly, the ID tags help store owners track new shipments. **Lastly,** / **Second,** these devices help cut down on theft.

4. To begin, some people worry that companies are tracking customers with the spy chips in order to get personal information. **In addition,** / **Third,** the chips could pose a health risk.

5. Secondly, the chips in cell phones only track the phones, not the kids who own them. **Furthermore,** / **Lastly,** the chips only work when the phone is turned on. **Finally,** / **Second,** the chips only send information, not protect the children.

B. Put the sentences in order to make a logical paragraph. Add transition words to complete the sentences with blanks.

(A) These twelve pyramids are useful for different ages and body types.

(B) _____, the government has a website for people to find the right pyramid for them.

(C) These new personal pyramids differ in three main ways from the old pyramids.

(D) _____, there are no more levels in each pyramid.

(E) Personal pyramids show people how much and what to eat.

(F) _____, now there are twelve pyramids.

(G) The food categories are now arranged side by side instead of top to bottom.

Order: ___, ___, ___, ___, ___, ___, ___

Unit 11 Worksheet: Simple Present, Simple Past, and *Used to*

The simple present tense is used to indicate that an action or state is repeated or usual in the present. The simple past is used to indicate that an action or state started and finished in the past. *Used to* is used to indicate an action or state that was repeated or usual over a period of time in the past, but it is not repeated or usual in the present. The negative form of *used to* is *did not use to*. The question form is *did + subject + use to*.

Examples
I **play** video games. I **am** not a criminal.
Criminals **existed** before video games.
People **used to be** more peaceful.
They **didn't use to play** violent video games.
Continental glaciers **used to cover** most of North America.

A. **Put a check (✓) beside the sentence that uses the correct verb form and a cross (✗) if it does not.**

   1. I usually practice the piano on Tuesday afternoons. _____
   2. When I was a kid, I behave badly at school. _____
   3. Yesterday, he did poorly on his test, and argued with his brother. _____
   4. They didn't use to sell clothes in this supermarket, but they do now. _____
   5. Sometimes, my parents help me with my homework. _____
   6. Last weekend, my uncle gets an award from the city. _____
   7. Did your grandparents used to play video games when they were kids? _____
   8. They live in the big gray house at the end of street. _____

B. **Complete the sentences with the correct form of the verb given.**

   1. The bottoms of glaciers _____ the Earth. (wear away)
   2. Today, continental glaciers _____ in the coldest places on Earth. (exist)
   3. Families _____ each other with daily problems, but they don't any more. (help)
   4. People _____ their bed sheets by hand, but now many people _____ a washing machine. (wash, use)
   5. We _____ a fascinating program about glaciers on TV last night. (see)
   6. Didn't the landscape around here _____ much different when we were kids? (be)

C. **Answer the questions with complete sentences.**

   1. What food do you like to eat now, but didn't use to?

      _____

   2. What activity or game did you use to like, but don't now?

      _____

   3. What do you usually do on Saturday nights?

      _____

Unit 12 Worksheet: Transitions for Time and Sequence

Transitional sequence words can be used to signify the chronological, or time, sequence of events. Time sequence words can be used to show absolute order (e.g. *first*, *second*, *third*, *next*, *then*, and *last*) or relative order (e.g. *before*, *after*, *while*, and *during*). Relative order shows events in relation to another event.

Examples
First, Bill Haley and the Comets recorded "Rock Around the Clock."
Second, Alan Freed coined the term "Rock 'n' Roll."
Third, Elvis Presley released his first record.

Alan Freed coined the term "Rock 'n' Roll."
Before that, Bill Haley and the Comets recorded "Rock Around the Clock."
Afterward, Elvis Presley released his first record.

A. Complete the sentences with a sequence word from the box.

first	third	before	after	then	during	last

1. Jim ate an entire pizza all by himself. _____ that, he had a stomachache.
2. First, you should learn a second language. _____, you'll be able to get into a better college.
3. _____ Jill bought her new shoes, she borrowed money from her mother.
4. First, Elvis made a record. Second, he performed his songs live in concert. _____, he became known as the king of Rock 'n' Roll.
5. _____ the last ice age, huge sheets of ice covered most of the Northern Hemisphere.
6. Last night, Gail's sister made a cake. _____, she mixed the ingredients. Then, she put the cake in the oven until it was cooked. _____, she decorated it with icing.

B. Use the sequence words to put the sentences in the correct order.

1. _____, he escaped slavery.
   _____, his words helped end slavery in the US.
   Frederick Douglass wrote an important autobiography.
   (before that, after that)

   _____

   _____

2. _____, it was banned in 1865.
   _____, slavery began in the US in the 1600s.
   _____, African Americans gained more equality in the 1900s.
   _____, unfair Jim Crow laws were made in the Southern US.
   (first, second, third, last)

   _____

   _____

   _____

   _____

Writing Feedback and Evaluation Form

The response...	0	1	2	3	4
CONTENT addresses the question or prompt well					
is organized					
has relevant details					
shows clear connections between ideas					
LANGUAGE uses accurate grammar					
uses appropriate vocabulary					
uses accurate spelling and punctuation					

Total: _____ /28

Basic Skills for the TOEFL® iBT 1

Jeff Zeter

Writing

Transcript & Answer Key

Transcript

[Unit 1]

Practice

M: OK, so southern states adopted two new laws that mainly affected African Americans: the poll tax laws and the Jim Crow laws. These laws did not support equal rights. Let's talk about what these laws were. **(Practice A ends.)** First, there were new poll tax laws. People now had to pay a seemingly small tax to vote. It was very little. Still it stopped a lot of people from voting. Fifty-percent-fewer African Americans voted in one state because of this tax. Second, Jim Crow laws were made. The laws made it OK to have separate areas for people. The areas were supposed to be equal. But they weren't. African Americans couldn't eat in the same areas as others. They couldn't use the same bathrooms. They weren't permitted to use the same front door. They would be arrested if they did.

Test

W: OK, let's talk about how Jim Crow laws started. They first began after the Supreme Court took away a law known as the Civil Rights Act of 1875. This law gave people social freedom. The court threw out this law. After it was gone, the Southern states started adopting lots of Jim Crow laws. For instance, African Americans couldn't ride in the same train cars with other people. They were arrested if they did. This happened to Homer Plessy. He went to court. The court said it was OK for him to have to sit in a separate train car because the train car was equal to the others.

[Unit 2]

Practice

W: OK. So, from the reading passage it seems like no one liked Picasso's art. This wasn't true. Lots of people did. **(Practice A ends.)** For instance, he had many fans from the start. They appreciated the unusual beauty in his paintings. Take Picasso's Boy with a Pipe. It's a painting of a poor, sad boy. This work sold quickly. And it has been resold. Many times! A family recently paid 104 million dollars for it. Many art critics also liked Picasso. A man named Apollinaire was one of them. Some said he was the most important art critic of the era. He was one of the first to notice Picasso's talent.

Test

M: Now let's talk about why this period really started. First, Picasso's closest friend died tragically. Picasso no longer appreciated life in the same way. He began to see sadness all around him. So he chose to paint it. He painted poor people on the streets. He even painted sad people in jail. Second, Picasso was alone and poor during this time. He was living away from home for the first time. Sometimes he didn't have money to buy paint. But, these hard years didn't last. He had many happier periods later. He was just sad and lonely during this brief era of his life.

[Unit 3]

Practice

M: Let's talk about a tiger's carnivore traits. First, tigers have very sharp claws. A tiger's claws are five inches (that's almost 13 centimeters) long. They are also shaped like hooks. **(Practice A ends.)** A tiger strikes its prey with these claws. Then the prey cannot escape. Tigers also have sharp teeth. These teeth are ten times bigger than a human's teeth are. These kill with just one bite. Now, a tiger has a simple stomach. It's not split into different parts like that of a plant-eating animal. Also, a tiger's digestive tract is only five times the length of its body. A plant-eating animal's is twenty-seven times longer than its body.

Test

W: OK. Some carnivores have become plant-eaters. A panda is a good example. Long ago, pandas ate mainly meat. Today, their instinct is to eat bamboo. They use their strong jaws to crush bamboo stems. They use their sharp teeth to pull it down and bite it off. They also use their teeth to pull off the outward part of the plant. But a panda's short digestive tract and stomach are made for meat. So, a panda doesn't digest bamboo well. It has only one stomach for food storage. It only digests twenty percent of what it eats. Therefore, pandas have to eat for sixteen hours a day.

[Unit 4]

Practice

W: OK. We know that prisms change the direction of light. Let's talk about two places we see this every day. First, we see this on sunny days. Think of the colors in the sky during a sunset. *(Practice A ends.)* There are reds, pinks, and oranges. This is because the atmosphere scatters the blue light waves away from the Earth. This leaves red, yellow, and orange. Second, we can see light changing direction on rainy days. A rainbow is caused by light shining through raindrops. Plain white sunlight enters each raindrop. The raindrop acts like a prism and splits the light into colors. Rainbows are composed this way.

Test

M: So there are some types of light that cannot be seen by humans. The spectrum is composed of millions of colors. But we can't see all of them. The average person can still see about one million different shades. Two to three percent of women can see many more colors—tens of millions more! In addition, humans cannot see ultra-violet light from the sun. These UV waves are shorter than white light waves. But guess what? This UV light can be seen by some other living things. Birds' and bees' eyes are different. Both can see UV light!

[Unit 5]

Practice

M: There are problems with franchises. Real problems. The first is cost. Running them is expensive. You've got to pay a "franchise fee." This is expensive. For example, take McDonalds. Its franchise fee can be over a million dollars. The second is no freedom. *(Practice A ends.)* There's no freedom to change things. OK, an example: Do you know Farrells' ice-cream shops? They were made to look old fashioned. This style was popular. But styles changed. People didn't like the old style and the owners could not change things! This would break the contract. As a result, many went out of business. Owning a franchise isn't always good.

Test

W: Did you know a famous name can be a bad thing? Here are two examples. First, one bad product can hurt many franchises. In 2001, many accidents were caused by problems with Goodyear tires. Only one type was the problem. Still, sales of all Goodyear tires dropped. Store owners who sold these tires lost money. Second, a business mistake made by one can hurt everyone. In 1993, four children died from eating undercooked hamburgers. This was at Jack in the Box. Many people stopped eating at all Jack in the Boxes. Thousands of owners lost profits. They were serving safe food. But having the same name was costly.

[Unit 6]

Practice

W: Many people once thought the Fission Theory made sense. But this explanation does not make sense today. There are a few reasons why. *(Practice A ends.)* First, it claims that the moon is a piece of Earth ripped away from the Pacific Ocean. But the oldest rocks from the ocean and rocks from the moon have been compared. Guess what. They are formed out of different chemicals. Second, the Earth couldn't have spun fast enough. If the moon was joined to the Earth, it would have spun four times faster. Still, scientists say that the rate would have been much too slow for a big mass to separate from the Earth.

Test

M: OK. How do we know that volcanoes did not make the craters on the moon? Why isn't this explanation a good one? Well, a group went to study the moon's surface. They discovered two things. First, the craters are perfect circles. Volcanic eruptions don't leave behind a design like this. Scientists now think that big chunks of space rock called meteorites crashed into the moon. This left the big craters. Also, they learned that the craters were older than the volcanoes. This proved that the volcanoes formed in the craters. The volcanoes didn't make the craters. You see, the craters were there first.

[Review 1]

Integrated 1

M: OK, so we know the constellations are helpful for remembering the stars. But why would people give them names? The stars add such beauty to the night sky. People have felt a need to create interesting stories and legends. These stories are an explanation as to where these "pictures" in the sky came from. These legends were also very useful to farmers. In some places, the seasons are very similar. Some historians suspect that the constellations were guidance to farmers. Because constellations appear at the same place each year, it would suggest to the farmers that it was time for the harvest or other events. This dependence on the sky became a strong part of many cultures.

Integrated 2

W: Let's talk about World War II. It is the most tragic war humanity has ever seen. The total loss of life reached over seventy million people. It was the most difficult war to settle. The Holocaust was one of the most severe chapters of the War. Almost six million Jews were murdered. Nazis were responsible for this. This was also the most expensive war ever. Major cities had been badly bombed. Supplies of all kinds had been limited throughout the War. Many people had been displaced. The situation took a long time to improve.

[Unit 7]

Practice

W: OK class. Frederick Douglass was born in the 1800s. He wrote an autobiography. It's a very important book. Why? It helped end slavery in the United States. *(Practice A ends.)* You see, Frederick Douglass was a slave. He had a terrible life. But he escaped. Next, he wrote his autobiography. Lots of people read it. So, how did it help end slavery? Well, it helped in two ways. First, it made people think about slavery. Many people did not know what it was like. It raised their awareness. Second, it gave other slaves the courage to speak out. They gave talks and wrote books. Frederick Douglass inspired them.

Test

M: OK memoirs... Anne Frank lived in Europe. She was a teenage girl. She was the author of a famous memoir. It is called *The Diary of Anne Frank*. Why is it important? First of all, it describes World War II. Anne's family was Jewish. They had to hide during the war. They hid for years. Finally, they were caught. But Anne Frank wrote all about it. The diary was published years later. It has a lot of history. Second, it tells about the terrible things that happened during the war. She explains what she went through. She talks about the evils of war. Many people read the Diary of Anne Frank. They think she was very wise. And they admire her for her courage. They also learn a lot about World War II.

[Unit 8]

Practice

M: OK. Let me just say that CO_2 created by nature is not the big problem. Man-made CO_2 is the real problem. **(Practice A ends.)** There are two reasons why. First of all, driving cars creates a lot of CO_2. CO_2 is released when cars burn fuel. US drivers released 314 million tons of CO_2 into the air in 2004. That's just a small part of all the Earth's vehicles. Power plants are another huge source of CO_2. The CO_2 given off by one forest fire is tiny compared to how much power plants produce. Coal-burning power plants in the US give off 1.5 billion tons of CO_2 annually.

Test

W: Do you think that cows cause a lot of pollution? I don't think so, but let's talk about it. First, methane gas that cows produce can be reduced. Scientists have found out how. A natural chemical is now being given to cows. This reduces the methane in their burps by seventy percent. So, the burping problem is easy to fix. Second, many people think that cow waste doesn't give off much methane gas. That's why scientists are focusing on burping. Besides, cow waste is natural. Maybe we should leave the cows alone. We should focus on reducing pollution from our vehicles and power plants instead!

[Unit 9]

Practice

W: OK. Let's talk about what each level of the food pyramid is. First, the bottom level refers to the main part of a healthy diet. It shows that bread, cereal, and pasta are most important. Six to eleven servings of these is recommended. Next is for fruits and vegetables. **(Practice A ends.)** Only two to five servings of these is suggested. Also, two to three servings of milk, cheese or yogurt should be eaten a day. The same is true for meat, beans, and nuts. Finally, we come to the top level of the pyramid. This shows that we should eat very little sugar or fat. So, it's OK to eat lots of oatmeal. But don't eat lots of oatmeal cookies!

Test

M: OK. Let's talk about how the new system is different. There are three main differences. First, there are now twelve pyramids. So, there are different pyramids for different people. Second, there are no more levels. The food sections are split in a new way. They are not divided from top to bottom! The food categories are now side by side. Finally, the government has a website. People can use it to find their own diagram. These personal pyramids show people what and how much to eat. Their personal pyramid is based on their age, gender, height, and weight. The new pyramids even suggest how much exercise each person should get.

[Unit 10]

Practice

M: OK. So stores say spy chips are good. But many people think they are not. Why? There are two reasons. The first is privacy. Some people think that companies are tracking customers, not shipments, with these devices. *(Practice A ends.)* They do this to get personal information. Then they use it to create new ways to sell more products. Second, the chips could be a health risk. They're sewn into clothes to prevent theft. Right? But the chips and readers emit electromagnetic energy. No one knows how safe this is. People don't want to wear something that is a health risk. So, some have stopped buying things with tags.

Test

W: So it seems that parents like this new spy technology. They feel it helps protect their kids. But it really doesn't make kids much safer. Here's why. First, chips in cell phones only track phones. If the teen isn't carrying the phone, the parent can't find the teen. Also, this technology only works if the cell phone is on. The parent can't track the child if the phone is off. Second, chips in cars only give parents information. They warn a parent if a teen is driving poorly. But they can't protect a teen from being in an accident.

[Unit 11]

Practice

W: Continental glaciers are fascinating. Why? Because they're so different from other glaciers. It's hard to imagine their scale and power. First, their scale. Here's an example; there's a sheet of ice that covers eighty-five percent of Greenland. It's three kilometers thick at certain points. *(Practice A ends.)* That's a big glacier. Antarctica also has glaciers this size. What would happen if they melted? The Earth's oceans would rise sixty meters! Second of all, these ice sheets are powerful. Their bottoms wear away the Earth. They can change the face of the Earth. The Great Lakes of the US all sit in big bowls or basins. These bowls were made by continental glaciers.

Test

M: OK. So, the world's glaciers are disappearing. This is not good. Not good at all. But sadly, it's true. I'll give you two examples. The Bering Glacier of Alaska is disappearing. This is because of global warming. It is the largest in North America. But, it is getting one kilometer smaller every year! This has been happening since 1990. Another example is the glacier on Mount Kilimanjaro. The landscape there has changed. This is because of farmers. They have cut and burnt nearby forests. Without the trees, the glacier on the mountain is in trouble. It's melting away. And, it's breaking off in huge pieces!

[Unit 12]

Practice

W: Right. Elvis didn't truly start Rock 'n' Roll. There are two reasons why. First, one of the biggest hits in Rock 'n' Roll was recorded before Elvis's first record. It was "Rock Around the Clock" by Bill Haley and the Comets. *(Practice A ends.)* This was in July of 1955. Many say this is the true start of Rock 'n' Roll. Second, a radio DJ named Alan Freed brought Rock 'n' Roll to audiences before Elvis. Freed even came up with the name "Rock 'n' Roll." In 1951, he had a nightly radio show. He called it Rock 'n' Roll Party. This was three years before Elvis's first record! Alan Freed also produced the first Rock 'n' Roll concerts in the country.

Test

M: OK. Here is another opinion about where Rock 'n' Roll came from. Many people believe the Rock 'n' Roll phenomenon came from rockabilly music. Rockabilly was fast-paced country rock music. It was popular in the early 50s. This was just before Rock 'n' Roll. Rock 'n' Roll grew from the fast beat of this music. Rockabilly artists were early icons of Rock 'n' Roll. Elvis performed with rockabilly musicians. This was before people knew his name. Wanda Jackson is one example. She was a famous rockabilly singer. So, you see Rock 'n' Roll may have come from rockabilly, not the blues.

[Review 2]

Integrated 1

M: OK, technology has changed how we use money. Not many people in the US carry a lot of cash anymore. Most people keep their money in a bank and use an ATM card to take money out. Some even use credit cards. However, there is a new phenomenon coming to the US. Soon many of us will never need to take cash out. We may not even carry a credit card! All we will need is our cell phones! Some countries already have systems where you can use a cell phone to pay for things. You go to a shop, buy a candy bar or even a computer, and pay for it just by scanning your cell phone! No cash, no ATM, and no credit card! Easy huh!

Integrated 2

W: Some people only listen to music that is on the charts. Do you see the problem with that? You only hear pop music that way. If the artist is not famous or doesn't have a lot of money, then they probably won't be on the charts. Awareness of what other music is out there is at an all time low. Some music that isn't on the charts would be very popular but no one hears it! You should give all kinds of music a chance. Maybe you will find something new you like. Here's one more thing to think about. It is hard for unknown artists to become known, especially if they are not signed with a record label. It is often the record labels that decide what will be on the charts. So, we have to demand more variety.

Answer Key

[Unit 1]

Independent

Getting Ready

Page 15

B

1. I <u>went on vacation</u> with my family.
2. We did this because <u>we like going to the beach together every year</u>.
3. My family <u>loved going to the beach together</u>.
4. I think that <u>this vacation was important to my family because it gave us time to relax together</u>.

Practice

Page 16

B

(B) Disagree

C

Topic: Family is <u>just as</u> important now.
A. Kids need more <u>support than ever</u>.
   1. Tried out for youth Olympic <u>soccer team</u>
   2. Would not have made the team <u>without family support</u>
B. Families offer lots of <u>guidance</u>.
   1. Kids make more bad <u>choices today</u>
   2. Kids need loving families to <u>guide them</u>
Conclusion: I believe families are <u>more important now</u>.

D

First
Also
Therefore

Page 17

E

(A) Agree

F

Topic: Family is <u>less</u> important now.
A. Family members do not seem to care about <u>being together</u>.
   1. Grandparents had a firm rule about <u>eating dinner together</u>.
   2. Today, mom and dad aren't home <u>at the same time</u>.
B. Family members do not <u>help each other</u>.
   1. Families used to stay together to <u>take care of each other</u>.
   2. Mom and her brother <u>live far from each other</u>.
Conclusion: For these reasons, I think family <u>is less important now</u>.

G

To begin with
For example
Also
As a result
For these reasons

H

1. guidance   2. Faith   3. competition
4. Severe   5. firm

Test

Page 18

Sample Answer 1
Agree
Topic: Family is <u>less</u> important now.
A. <u>Families are not as close as they used to be</u>.
   1. <u>My parents don't think it is important to see each other on holidays</u>.
   2. <u>We don't see each other for months</u>.
B. <u>Grandmother still likes getting all her family together</u>.
   1. <u>She is firm about us being together on Christmas and birthdays</u>.
   2. <u>Mom does not think it is as important</u>.
Conclusion: This is why I feel that family is <u>less important now than it was in the past</u>.

I think that family is <u>less</u> important now than it was in the past. I think this because <u>families are not as close as they used to be</u>. For example, <u>my parents do not think it is important to see each other on holidays. As a result, we sometimes don't see each other for months</u>. I also believe this because <u>my grandmother still likes getting the whole family together</u>. For example, <u>she is firm about us being together on Christmas and birthdays</u>. However, <u>my mom does not think it is as important. My mom still has faith in me, but I don't see her very often</u>. This is why I feel that family is <u>less important now than it was in the past</u>.

Sample Answer 2
Disagree
Topic: Family is <u>just as</u> important now.
A. <u>Many moms still stay at home</u>.
   1. <u>My mom feels that taking care of her family is most important</u>.
   2. <u>My mom offers us guidance</u>.
B. <u>Many dads take time off from work</u>.
   1. <u>My dad watches my soccer competitions</u>.
   2. <u>My dad spends time with me during vacations</u>.
Conclusion: This is why I feel that family is <u>just as important now as it was in the past</u>.

I think that family is <u>just as</u> important now as it was in the past. I think this because <u>many moms still stay at home to look after their kids</u>. For example, <u>my mom did not get a job. She feels that taking care of her family is most important and she wants to offer us guidance if we need it</u>. I also believe this because <u>nowadays many dads take time off from work to be with their kids</u>. For example, <u>my dad takes time off from work so he can watch my soccer competitions. He also takes time off during my school vacations to spend time with me</u>. This is why I feel that family is <u>just as important now as it was in the past</u>.

Integrated

Getting Ready

Page 19

B

1. A
2. They might talk about who made these laws, if people thought these laws were good, and what the effects were on African Americans.

Practice

Page 20

A

(A)

B

Reading

Main idea: The effects of two types <u>of new laws on African Americans</u>

Key points:
- The laws did not support <u>equal rights</u>
- African Americans did not have <u>political freedom</u>
  - Many African Americans could not afford to <u>vote</u>
- The laws did not give African Americans <u>social freedom</u>
  - African Americans could not use <u>the same areas as others</u>

Lecture

Main idea: New laws <u>did not support African Americans' equal rights</u>

Key points:
- Poll taxes stopped many African Americans from <u>voting</u>
  - Fifty-percent-fewer <u>in one state voted</u>
- Jim Crow laws made it OK to <u>have separate areas</u>
  - The areas were supposed to be <u>equal but weren't</u>

Page 21

D

The reading explains how <u>laws adopted</u> in the American South did not support equal rights for African Americans. These laws <u>did not allow</u> political or social freedoms. The lecture illustrates how this was true.

The speaker says that poll taxes kept African Americans from voting. The speaker says that in one state <u>fifty-percent-fewer</u> African Americans voted because of these taxes.

The speaker also explains that Jim Crow laws unfairly separated African Americans from other people. The areas <u>were supposed to be</u> separate but equal. However, they were not. African Americans could not use the same nice areas as others.

E

1. social   2. adopt   3. permit
4. legal   5. arrests

Test

Page 22

Step 1

Reading

Main idea: The Supreme Court permitted African Americans to be treated unfairly.

Key points:
- Court took away the <u>Civil Rights Act of 1875</u>
  - This law had allowed all people to <u>use the areas they wanted</u>
- Court made it legal to allow separate but <u>equal places</u>

Lecture

Main idea: How Jim Crow laws first started.
Key points:
- After Civil Rights Act of 1875 was gone, southern states <u>started adopting lots of Jim Crow laws</u>
  - African Americans couldn't <u>ride in the same trains</u>
- Homer Plessy went <u>to court</u>
  - They said it was OK for him <u>to sit in a separate train</u>

Page 23

Step 3

Topic: The reading and the lecture are about the removal of the Civil Rights Act of 1875 and the start of <u>the Jim Crow Laws.</u>

A. The Supreme Court permitted <u>African Americans to be treated unfairly.</u>
   1. They removed the <u>Civil Rights Act.</u>
   2. They made it legal to allow separate <u>but equal areas.</u>

B. Southern states started adopting <u>lots of Jim Crow laws.</u>
  1. African Americans couldn't ride <u>in the same trains as other people.</u>
  2. The court said it was OK for Homer Plessy to <u>sit in a separate train.</u>
Conclusion: The lecture supports the reading because it gives examples of how these laws allowed African Americans to be treated unfairly.

Step 4

The reading and the lecture are about <u>the removal of the Civil Rights Act of 1875 and the start of the Jim Crow Laws.</u> The reading says that the Supreme Court permitted African Americans to be treated unfairly by <u>removing the Civil Rights Act and by making it legal to allow separate but equal areas for people.</u>

The lecture explains that after this, southern states started adopting lots of Jim Crow laws. For example, <u>African Americans couldn't ride in the same trains as other people.</u> The lecture also talks about Homer Plessy who went to court. The court said <u>it was OK for him to sit in a separate train.</u>

The lecture supports the reading because <u>it gives examples of how these laws allowed African Americans to be treated unfairly.</u>

Check-up

Page 24

1. offer
2. vote
3. future
4. seemingly
5. tax
6. As a result

[Unit 2]

Independent

Getting Ready

Page 25

B
1. It was <u>my aunt Denise.</u>
2. He/she taught me <u>how to make brownies.</u>
3. I felt <u>it was fun because I like brownies, and Denise makes them really well.</u>
4. He/she was <u>patient with me and let me do all the mixing.</u>

Practice

Page 26

B
(A) Agree

C
Topic: Parents <u>do</u> make the best teachers.
A. Parents know you <u>the best.</u>
  1. They know
   • the things you do <u>well</u>
   • your <u>flaws</u>
  2. Takes a teacher a long time to notice that
   • you can <u>multiply big numbers</u>
   • you find geometry <u>hard</u>
B. Parents know how to keep kids <u>interested.</u>
  1. Dad lets me <u>build my math problems</u>
  2. I like to make models of <u>math problems</u>
Conclusion: I feel that parents are <u>great teachers.</u>

D
First of all
The second reason
For example

Page 27

E
(B) Disagree

F
Topic: Parents <u>do not</u> make the best teachers.
A. Teachers have been <u>trained</u> to teach, parents haven't.
  1. Teachers went to <u>college to learn how to teach.</u>
  2. Parents have other <u>jobs.</u>
  3. My father knows a lot about science, but not <u>about geometry.</u>
B. Teachers treat students the same.
  1. Parents wouldn't be <u>fair.</u>
  2. Mom would expect me to be <u>perfect.</u>
Conclusion: Parents <u>should not</u> be teachers.

G
First of all
However
Secondly
For example

H
1. perfect
2. hardly
3. relatives
4. multiply
5. flaw

Test

Page 28

Sample Answer 1
Agree
Topic: Parents <u>do</u> make the best teachers.
A. <u>My mom is a perfect teacher.</u>
  1. <u>She taught me how to read and ride my bike.</u>
  2. <u>She knows a lot.</u>

B. She was the best teacher.
  1. She was patient.
  2. She made it fun.
Conclusion: I think that parents are the best teachers.

I think that parents do make the best teachers. This is because my mom is a perfect teacher. An example is that she taught me to how to read. She also taught me how to ride my bike. She is a good teacher because she is a lawyer, so she knows a lot. In my experience, she was the best teacher. She was patient and let me take my time. She made sure I was not going to fail. She made it fun to learn. She made up games to help me learn to multiply. For these reasons, I think that parents are the best teachers.

Sample Answer 2
Disagree
Topic: Parents do not make the best teachers.
A. Parents hardly remember what they learned in school.
  1. My dad did not know how to do the math problems.
  2. My dad didn't remember the math he learned at school.
B. Parents do not know all the stuff I need to learn.
  1. Parents did not train to become teachers.
  2. My mom has never been good at science.
Conclusion: I think that parents do not make the best teachers.

I think that parents do not make the best teachers. This is because they hardly remember what they learned in school. An example is my dad. I asked him to help me with my math homework, and he did not know how to do the problems. He said he could not remember the math he learned when he was at school. In my experience, parents do not know all the stuff I need to learn. They did not go to school to train to become teachers. My mom has never been good at science. She said it is one of her flaws. For these reasons, I think that parents do not make the best teachers.

Integrated

Getting Ready
Page 29
B
1. B
2. They might talk about who didn't like Picasso's work, other reasons why people didn't like Picasso's work, and how Picasso's work made people feel.

Practice
Page 30
A
(A)

B
Reading
Main idea: Reasons why people did not like Picasso's art.
Key points:
- Picasso's art seemed tragic
  - People looked sad and poor
- Picasso's art did not look real
  - He used squares and triangles for people's shapes

Lecture
Main idea: There were many people who liked Picasso's art
Key points:
- Picasso had many fans from the start
- Many people liked the unusual beauty
  - *Boy with a Pipe* sold for 104 million dollars
- Many critics also liked Picasso
  - Apollinaire was the most important art critic of the time
  - He was one of the first to notice Picasso's talent

Page 31
D
The reading explains why people did not like Picasso's tragic art. They did not like how he made people look sad and poor. They also did not like his style of cubism.

The lecture shows that many people really did think that Picasso was a great artist. The speaker says that many fans appreciated Picasso's work. The speaker says one painting sold for 104 million dollars.

The speaker also says that many art critics liked Picasso's art as well. A very important critic, Apollinaire, noticed Picasso's great talent first. The lecture shows that many people did like Picasso.

E
1. era   2. imitate   3. humanity
4. tragic   5. appreciate

Test

Page 32

Step 1

Reading

Main idea: Picasso's _blue period_

Key points:
- Picasso did not like <u>the politics of the era</u>
- Picasso felt that poor people <u>were not treated well</u>
- Picasso's self-portrait shows that he was <u>an unhappy artist</u>
  - In his self-portrait, he looks <u>pale, sad, and older</u>

Lecture

Main idea: The real causes for Picasso's <u>blue period</u>

Key points:
- One of Picasso's close friends <u>died during this time</u>
- Picasso no longer <u>appreciated life</u>
- Picasso was alone and <u>poor</u>
  - He lived away from home <u>for the first time</u>

Page 33

Step 3

Topic: The reading and the lecture are about Picasso's <u>blue period</u>.

A. The reading says his blue period started because
  1. he did not like <u>the politics of the era</u>
  2. he thought poor people were <u>not treated well</u>
  3. he was an unhappy artist as shown in his <u>self-portrait</u>

B. The lecture says his blue period started because
  1. his good <u>friend died</u>
  2. he was poor and living away from <u>home for the first time</u>

Conclusion: The lecture challenges the reading by offering different causes for Picasso's blue period.

Step 4

The reading and the lecture are about <u>Picasso's blue period</u>. The reading says that the blue period happened because Picasso did not like <u>the politics of the era</u>. It says he thought <u>poor people were not treated well</u>. The reading also says Picasso was an <u>unhappy artist</u> because he looked very unhappy in <u>his self-portrait painted during this time</u>.

However, the lecture gives another reason for how <u>Picasso's blue period started</u>. The speaker challenges the reading by saying that Picasso's good friend <u>dying and being poor and living away from home were the reasons his blue period began</u>.

The lecture challenges the reading by <u>offering different causes for Picasso's blue period</u>.

Page 34

1. Cubism   2. unusual   3. train
4. fans   5. lawyer   6. secretary

[Unit 3]

Independent

Getting Ready

Page 35

B
1. The thing I do is <u>buy a lot of shoes</u>.
2. I do this because <u>I like to wear a different pair of shoes every day</u>.
3. I think that it <u>makes people notice me</u>.
4. I think that <u>I do care too much</u>. Therefore, I should <u>not spend so much money on shoes</u>.

Practice

Page 36

B
(A) Agree

C

Topic: People <u>do care too much</u> about appearance and fashion.

A. People buy <u>popular clothes</u>.
  1. People think clothes <u>reflect who they are</u>.
  2. My friend spends money on <u>trendy clothes</u>.
B. People are too self-<u>conscious</u>.
  1. My friend wears <u>high heels</u>.
    • They hurt <u>her feet</u>.
    • She thinks <u>they look good</u>.
  2. My friend reads too many <u>beauty magazines</u>.
Conclusion: I think people are happier when <u>they do not worry about fashion and appearance</u>.

D
Also
However
Therefore

Page 37

E
(B) Disagree

F

Topic: People <u>do not care too much</u> about appearance and fashion.

A. It is good to <u>care about beauty</u>.
  1. People should want to look <u>good</u>.
  2. I care about <u>how I look</u>.

I Answer Key I   **11**

Answer Key

B. People like to wear nice <u>clothes</u>.
  1. Some clothes are <u>made well</u>.
  2. I wear popular <u>brands because I like the clothes</u>.
Conclusion: I am conscious of how I look, but <u>I do not think about it all the time</u>.

G
First
Also
However

H
1. worth   2. reflect   3. brand
4. Beauty   5. conscious

Test

Page 38

Sample Answer 1
Agree
Topic: I <u>think</u> people care too much about appearances.
A. <u>People care too much about how they look</u>.
  1. <u>They change their hairstyle every week</u>.
  2. <u>They want to look like famous people</u>.
B. <u>People care too much about being trendy</u>.
  1. <u>They only buy clothes from one brand</u>.
  2. <u>They think the clothes will make them popular</u>.
Conclusion: This is why I <u>think people care too much</u> about appearances and fashion.

I <u>think</u> people care too much about appearances. First, I think <u>people care too much about how they look</u>. For example, <u>some people care too much about their hair. They change their hairstyle every week. Sometimes they want to look like the famous people in magazines. My friend Jill is never happy with her hair</u>. Second, <u>people care too much about being trendy</u>. For example, <u>they only buy clothes from one brand. My friend John only buys clothes from one store. He thinks the clothes will make him popular</u>. This is why I <u>think people care too much</u> about appearances and fashion.

Sample Answer 2
Disagree
Topic: I <u>don't think</u> people care too much about appearances.
A. <u>Beauty reflects who you are and doesn't hurt anyone</u>.
  1. <u>My mom puts on a lot of makeup</u>.
  2. <u>It makes her feel good</u>.
B. <u>Some clothing brands are better than others</u>.
  1. <u>I buy clothes from my favorite store</u>.
  2. <u>I like the way I look in their clothes</u>.
Conclusion: This is why I <u>don't think it is bad to care</u> about appearances and fashion.

I <u>don't think</u> people care too much about appearances. First, I think <u>it is OK that beauty is important to people. It reflects who you are and doesn't hurt anyone. For example, my mom puts on a lot of makeup. It makes her feel good</u>. Second, <u>it is OK to care about clothes. Some clothing brands are better than others, and I think it is worth paying more for them</u>. For example, <u>I am conscious of how I look. Therefore, I buy clothes from my favorite store. I like the way I look in clothes from that store. It makes me feel good about myself</u>. This is why I <u>don't think it is bad to care</u> about appearances and fashion.

Integrated

Getting Ready

Page 39

B
1. B
2. They might talk about the inside traits of a carnivore, a few different examples of carnivores, or why some animals are carnivores.

Practice

Page 40

A
(A)

B
Reading

Main idea: Carnivores are built for <u>eating meat</u>
Key points:
- A carnivore's outward traits <u>help them catch and chew animals</u>
  - They have <u>sharp claws and teeth</u>
- A carnivore's inside traits are made for <u>eating meat</u>
  - They have <u>simple stomachs</u>
  - Their digestive tracts are <u>shorter</u>

Lecture

Main idea: The carnivore traits of <u>a tiger</u>
Key points:
- A tiger's claws <u>are five inches long</u>
  - A tiger's teeth are ten times <u>bigger than a human's</u>
- A tiger's stomach <u>is not split</u>
- A tiger's digestive tract is <u>five times the length of its body</u>
  - A plant-eating animal's is <u>twenty-seven times longer than its body</u>

Page 41

D

The reading describes the outward and inside traits of a carnivore. These traits help a carnivore catch and eat animals. The lecture uses a tiger as an example to describe the traits of a carnivore. The speaker says that a tiger has sharp teeth and claws that it uses to catch and eat its prey. The speaker says a tiger's claws are five inches long. The speaker also describes the tiger's simple stomach and short digestive tract. Its digestive tract is only five times the length of its body. A plant-eating animal has a much longer digestive tract.

E

1. diet 2. trait 3. storage
4. instinct 5. strike

Test

Page 42

Step 1

Reading

Main idea: Animals can change from eating meat to eating plants.
Key points:
- Diet changed because there was not much prey left
- Animals use their carnivore traits to eat plants
  - They have a hard time digesting plants

Lecture

Main idea: Panda are carnivores that eat plants.
Key points:
- Pandas eat bamboo using their strong jaws and sharp teeth.
- A panda doesn't digest bamboo well.
  - It only digests twenty percent.
  - It eats for sixteen hours a day.

Page 43

Step 3

Topic: The reading and the lecture are about how an animal can change from being a plant eater to a meat eater.
A. The reading says
  1. that the animals changed because their diet changed
  2. they started using their carnivore traits
B. The lecture says
  1. this is true for the panda
  2. the panda uses its strong jaws and sharp teeth
C. The reading says that these animals have a hard time digesting plants.

D. The lecture says the panda does not digest bamboo well.
  1. It digests twenty percent of what it eats.
  2. It eats for sixteen hours a day.
Conclusion: The lecture supports the points made in the reading by using the panda as an example.

Step 4

The reading and the lecture are about how an animal can change from being a meat eater to a plant eater. The reading says that the animals changed because their diet changed. Therefore, they started using their carnivore traits to eat tough plants. The lecture discusses how this is true for the panda. The speaker says that the panda uses its strong jaws and sharp teeth to eat plants.

The reading says that these animals have a hard time digesting plants. The speaker also supports this by talking about how the panda does not digest bamboo well. It only digests twenty percent of what it eats, so it has to eat for sixteen hours a day.

The lecture supports the points made in the reading by using the panda as an example.

Check-up

Page 44

1. appearance 2. magazines 3. trendy
4. digestive 5. tract 6. outward

[Unit 4]

Independent

Getting Ready

Page 45

B

1. It was when I read a story about Christmas in front of the school for the Christmas play.
2. Because I tried out for the reading part and got it.
3. I felt that it was lots of fun and also a lot of work.
4. I think that it was good for me to practice talking in front of so many people.

Practice

Page 46

B

(B) Disagree

C

Topic: Writing well is not as important as speaking well.
A. First impressions are based on what you say.
  1. When you interview for a job you have to speak clearly.

2. When you interview for a job your responses can't be <u>one-word sentences</u>.
B. Must be able to speak well on the <u>phone</u>.
   1. People don't want to hear <u>mumbling on the phone</u>.
   2. You need to <u>convey what you want aloud</u>.
Conclusion: I believe <u>speaking well is more important than writing well</u>.

D
The first reason
For example
The second reason
Therefore

Page 47
E
(A) Agree

F
Topic: It is better to <u>write well than to speak well</u>.
A. To get a job you have to <u>write well</u>.
   1. You might have to write a <u>letter about work experience</u>.
   2. Writing poorly gives a <u>poor impression</u>.
B. Our culture uses <u>email</u>.
   1. You have to send <u>written messages</u>.
   2. You have to convey <u>your opinions clearly</u>.
Conclusion: I believe it is more important <u>to write well</u>.

G
First of all
Secondly
For example

H
1. impression   2. response   3. convey
4. interview   5. nervous

Test
Page 48
Sample Answer 1
Agree
Topic: I think it is better to <u>speak well</u>.
A. <u>More people hear what you say than read what you write</u>.
   1. <u>I never write to my family or friends</u>.
   2. <u>My teachers are the only people who read what I write</u>.
B. <u>Being a good speaker also gives a good impression</u>.
   1. <u>My friend John always gets the good parts in the school play</u>.
   2. <u>You do not do any writing in the school play</u>.
Conclusion: I think it is better to <u>speak well</u>.

I think it is better to <u>speak well</u>. This is because <u>people hear what you say more often than they read what you write</u>. For example, <u>I never write to my family or friends. My teachers are the only people who read what I write</u>. Another reason is <u>being a good speaker also gives a good impression</u>. An example is <u>in the school play. My friend John is good at speaking. He always gets the good parts. You do not do any writing in the school play because that would be boring</u>. For these reasons, I think it is better to <u>speak well than to write well</u>.

Sample Answer 2
Disagree
Topic: I think it is better to <u>write well</u>.
A. <u>To be more successful</u>
   1. <u>Good jobs require you to write well</u>.
   2. <u>Get a better grade if there are no sloppy mistakes</u>.
B. <u>To convey what we mean</u>
   1. <u>I get nervous speaking so I write letters or emails</u>.
   2. <u>More people write emails than call people</u>.
Conclusion: I think it is better to <u>write well</u>.

I think it is better to <u>write well</u>. This is because <u>my English teacher says we should learn to write well so that we will be more successful in life</u>. For example <u>in our culture, many good jobs require you to write well. I also have to write well in English class. I get a better grade if there are no sloppy mistakes</u>. Another reason is <u>that we have to convey what we mean clearly</u>. An example <u>of this is that I get nervous speaking to people, so I write letters or emails instead. I think this will be true too when I get a job. More people write emails than call</u>. For these reasons, I think it is better to <u>write well than to speak well</u>.

Integrated

Getting Ready
Page 49
B
1. A
2. They might talk about light, colors, or other things a prism does.

Practice
Page 50
A
(B)

B
Reading

Main idea: A prism's effect on colors and light.
Key points:
- A prism refracts light/changes the direction of light
- A prism bends the waves of light.

Lecture

Main idea: Everyday places that a prism changes light.
Key points:
- Can see it in the colors in the sky during a sunset
  - The atmosphere scatters the blue light
- Plain white light enters each raindrop
  - The raindrop acts like a prism and splits the light into colors
  - This is how a rainbow is composed

Page 51
D

The reading explains how a prism refracts and bends light. White light is changed as it goes through a prism. This causes the colors of the rainbow to come out the other side of the prism. The lecture explains how we can see this every day.

The speaker says that the atmosphere scatters the blue light in the sky to make the sunset look red, yellow, and orange. The speaker also explains that a rainbow is the result of a raindrop acting like a prism. A prism takes plain light and turns it into many beautiful colors.

E
1. experiment   2. waves   3. plain
4. composed   5. scattered

Test
Page 52
Step 1
Reading

Main idea: The color spectrum has two types of light
Key points:
- Plain white light is the type of light our eyes can see
- Other types of light cannot be seen by humans
  - An example is the light that causes sunburn

Lecture

Main idea: There are types of light that cannot be seen by humans
Key points:
- The spectrum is composed of millions of colors
- Humans can see about a million different shades of white light
  - Some women can see many more

- Humans cannot see UV light
  - Birds and bees can

Page 53
Step 3
Topic: The reading and the lecture are about the different types of light.
A. The reading discusses the two types of light in the color spectrum.
 1. Humans can only see white light.
 2. There are other types of light that the human eye cannot see.
  - The light that causes sunburns
B. The lecture discusses how the spectrum is composed of millions of colors.
 1. The average person can see about one million different colors.
  - Some women can see many more
 2. Humans cannot see ultra-violet light but birds and bees can.
Conclusion: The lecture supports the points made in the reading by giving examples of what light humans can and cannot see.

Step 4

The reading and the lecture are about the different types of light. The reading discusses the two types of light in the color spectrum. Humans can only see white light. However, there are many other types of light we cannot see such as the light that causes sunburn.

The lecture supports the reading by giving further information. The lecture discusses how the spectrum is composed of millions of colors. However, the average person can only see about one million different colors. However, some women can see many more. The speaker also gives an example of light that humans cannot see. This is ultra-violet light. However, birds and bees can see it.

The lecture supports the points made in the reading by giving examples of what light humans can and cannot see.

Check-up
Page 54

1. prism   2. aloud   3. spectrum
4. motion   5. mumble   6. pattern

Answer Key

[Unit 5]

Independent

Getting Ready

Page 55

B

1. The experience was <u>using a computer to send email</u>.
2. I needed to use the computer because <u>it can connect to the Internet, so I can check and send my email</u>.
3. <u>I could not have sent email without a computer</u>.
4. I think that <u>the computer made this experience very easy</u>.

Practice

Page 56

B

(B) Disagree

C

Topic: Computers <u>have not</u> made people's lives better.
A. Computers add <u>stress to our lives</u>.
   1. People get a lot of <u>spam</u>.
   2. Spam wastes company's <u>money</u>.
B. Computers can break and be <u>expensive to fix</u>.
   1. Computers cost a lot of money and <u>do not always work</u>.
   2. I have lost <u>homework</u>.
Conclusion: Computers just <u>cause too much stress</u>.

D

First
Also
Therefore

Page 57

E

(A) Agree

F

Topic: Computers have made our <u>lives better</u>.
A. Computers let people <u>communicate easily</u>.
   1. Can send messages to friends who <u>live far away</u>.
   2. Sending letters takes a <u>long time</u>.
B. The Internet makes it <u>easier to do many things</u>.
   1. People can find <u>information</u> and download <u>programs</u>.
   2. I use the <u>Internet</u> for homework, and <u>software</u> for essays.
Conclusion: Computers have <u>made my life better</u>.

G

To begin
Also
I also
Still

H

1. reach   2. deal with   3. download
4. software   5. stress

Test

Page 58

Sample Answer 1
Agree
Topic: I <u>think</u> computers have made people's lives better.
A. <u>We can communicate quicker</u>.
   1. <u>Email is faster than regular mail</u>.
   2. <u>Can use a messenger program to reach friends easily</u>.
B. <u>Computers save time</u>.
   1. <u>Using a keyboard is easier than using a pen and paper</u>.
   2. <u>Can save time writing essays</u>.
Conclusion: Without computers, <u>I think life would be a lot harder</u>.

I <u>think</u> computers have made people's lives better. I think this because <u>we can communicate quicker</u>. For instance, <u>email is faster than regular mail. I can also use a messenger program to reach my friends easily. I do not need to wait long for a reply</u>. I also think this because <u>computers save people time.</u>
For example, <u>using a keyboard is easier than using a pen and paper. I use my computer to write my essays. I can type faster than I can write. So I save time writing my essays</u>. Without computers, <u>I think life would be a lot harder</u>.

Sample Answer 2
Disagree
Topic: I <u>don't think</u> computers have made people's lives better.
A. <u>Computers cause us a lot of trouble and stress</u>.
   1. <u>They can often break</u>.
   2. <u>My computer will shut down suddenly</u>.
B. <u>Computers make people lazy</u>.
   1. <u>Some people sit in front of the computer all day</u>.
   2. <u>It is unhealthy</u>.
Conclusion: Without computers, <u>people would have fewer things to worry about</u>.

I don't think computers have made people's lives better. I think this because computers cause us a lot of trouble. They cause a lot of stress. For instance, computers can often break. Sometimes, my computer will shut down suddenly when I am downloading something. It makes me very angry, and I don't know how to deal with it. I also think this because computers make people lazy. For example, some people sit in front of the computer all day. This is bad for you. My dad uses the computer too much. I am worried that he is unhealthy. Without computers, people would have fewer things to worry about.

Integrated

Getting Ready

Page 59

B

1. A
2. They might talk about other benefits to owning a franchise, some franchises that have done really well, or how the owner can make and save money by owning a franchise.

Practice

Page 60

A

(B)

B

Reading

Main idea: The benefits of owning a franchise
Key points:
- A franchise can help owners save money
- Franchises give owners lots of freedom of choice

Lecture

Main idea: The problems with opening a franchise
Key points:
- Franchise owners have to pay a fee
- In franchises, there is no freedom to change things
  - Doing so would break the contract

Page 61

D

The reading explains how a franchise business allows one company to sell the products of another company through a joint contract. A franchise can help business owners save money and have freedom of choice.

The lecture, however, describes some problems of opening a franchise business. The speaker says that the franchise fee makes opening the business very expensive. Unlike what the reading says, the speaker also says that there is no freedom to change

things. If something is wrong, the franchise owner won't let the business owner change anything. This can make it very difficult to be successful.

E

1. benefit   2. right   3. joint
4. contract   5. profit

Test

Page 62

Step 1

Reading

Main idea: The benefits of two types of franchises.
Key points:
- A product-and-trade-name franchise allows the owner to make or sell a well-known product
- A business-format franchise gives the owner the right to use a well-known name

Lecture

Main idea: A well-known name can be a bad thing.
Key points:
- One bad product can hurt many franchises
  - Accidents were caused by Goodyear tires
  - Store owners lost money
- Business mistakes made by one business can hurt everyone
  - Children died from eating Jack in the Box
  - Thousands of owners lost profits

Page 63

Step 3

Topic: The reading and the lecture are about how a well-known name can either help or hurt a business.
A. The reading discusses the benefits of
  1. product-and-trade-name franchises
  2. business-format franchises
B. The lecture discusses how selling a well-known name or product can be a bad thing.
  1. Goodyear tires
    • They caused accidents.
  2. Jack in the Box restaurants
    • A few sold undercooked hamburgers.
  3. The owners lost money.
Conclusion: The lecture refutes the points made in the reading about the benefits of a brand name.

Step 4

The reading and the lecture are about how a well-known name can either help or hurt a business. The reading discusses the benefits of product-and-trade-name franchises and business-format franchises. They both offer benefits of well-known brand names or products.

Answer Key

The lecture refutes the reading by discussing how selling a well-known name or product can be a bad thing. Examples included Goodyear tires that were found to cause accidents and a few Jack in the Box restaurants that sold undercooked hamburgers. In both these cases, the owners of business that sold these lost money because they were selling a well-known brand.

Therefore, the lecture refutes the points made in the reading about the benefits of a brand name.

Check-up

Page 64

1. accidents
2. spam
3. costly
4. easily
5. tried-and-true
6. program

[Unit 6]

Independent

Getting Ready

Page 65

B

1. The experience was presenting my book report on *Island of the Blue Dolphin*.
2. I felt this way because my teacher said it was too good and someone older must have helped me with it, so she gave me a low grade.
3. No, I didn't because my feelings were so hurt.
4. I learned that teachers aren't always fair.

Practice

Page 66

B

(A) Agree

C

Topic: Students should grade their teachers.
A. Some teachers have been teaching for a long time.
   1. Teachers are used to doing things the same ways.
   2. Bad grades would help them improve.
B. Teachers could see how much they are appreciated.
   1. Students don't thank teachers for hard work.
   2. Giving high grades could be a good way to do this.
Conclusion: Hopefully, grading teachers would be good for everyone.

D

First of all
Second

Page 67

E

(B) Disagree

F

Topic: Students should not grade their teachers.
A. Teachers have already been to school.
   1. They were shown how to teach.
   2. They could not teach if they had not passed.
B. There is already a grading system for teachers.
   1. Principal checks that they are good at their job.
   2. Principal evaluates them every year.
   3. Principal has more experience in grading than students.
Conclusion: I do not believe that students should grade their teachers.

G

First
Second

H

1. fault
2. evaluate
3. remark
4. improve
5. continually

Test

Page 68

Sample Answer 1
Agree
Topic: I think that teachers should be graded.
A. It would be useful for them to remember what it feels like.
   1. I get nervous.
   2. I forget answers.
B. Teachers might find out how well the students are learning.
   1. It would help them be better teachers.
   2. It would help them see their own faults and be more understanding.
Conclusion: I think that teachers should be graded like we are.

I think that teachers should be graded. This is because it would be useful for them to remember what it feels like. For example, I get nervous when I know that my teacher is going to grade me. I continually forget the answers when I'm nervous. This is because I want to make sure that I get it right. I also think that teachers might find out how well the students are learning if someone were grading them. Hopefully, this would help them be better teachers. This would help them see their own faults and be more understanding of other people's. For these reasons, I think that teachers should be graded like we are.

Sample Answer 2
Disagree
Topic: I think that teachers <u>do not need to be graded</u>.
A. <u>They are already teachers.</u>
   1. <u>They have to pass a test to be a teacher.</u>
   2. <u>They get evaluated by the principal.</u>
B. <u>Only kids need to be graded.</u>
   1. <u>Grading us lets our teachers know if we need extra help.</u>
   2. <u>Grading our teachers won't help them.</u>
Conclusion: I think that teachers <u>do not need to be graded</u>.

    I think <u>that teachers do not need to</u> be graded. This is because <u>they are already teachers.</u> For example, <u>they have to pass a test to be a teacher. They get evaluated by the principal</u> every year too. <u>But they already know how to teach.</u> I also think that <u>only kids need to be graded because we still do not know how to do some things. Grading us lets our teachers know if we need extra help. We can't help our teachers by grading them.</u> This would help <u>only if teachers have to learn something new or improve their skills. But still it shouldn't be all students that grade them.</u> For these reasons, I think that teachers <u>do not need to be graded. Only students do</u>.

Integrated

Getting Ready

Page 69

B

1. B
2. They might talk about what The Fission Theory is, what the other idea for it was, or what the moon is made of.

Practice

Page 70

A

(B)

B

Reading

Main idea: The fission theory explains how <u>the moon was formed</u>.
Key points:
- The moon was <u>a piece of the Earth</u>
  - It came from <u>the Pacific Ocean</u>
- The Earth was spinning so fast it threw off the <u>large piece</u>
  - It began orbiting <u>the Earth</u>

Lecture

Main idea: The fission theory does not <u>make sense today</u>.
Key points:
- The rocks from the ocean and the moon are <u>formed out of different chemicals</u>
- The Earth couldn't have spun fast <u>enough to throw off a piece of it</u>

Page 71

D

    The reading discusses how <u>The Fission Theory</u> was the first to explain how the moon was formed. It stated that a piece of the Earth broke off and was pulled into the <u>Earth's orbit</u>. This piece became the moon.

    The lecture explains how this theory does not make sense today. The speaker says the rocks from the <u>Pacific Ocean</u> and the rocks on the moon are made of different chemicals.

    The speaker also says that the Earth could not have <u>spun fast enough</u> for a piece to break off and be pulled into orbit. If the moon was joined to the Earth, it would still spin too slowly for a piece to be thrown off.

E

1. explanation   2. theory   3. rate
4. claims   5. mass

Test

Page 72

Step 1

Reading

Main idea: People believed that volcanoes <u>caused the craters on the moon</u>.
Key points:
- Dark spots were made of <u>lava</u>.
- Moon's <u>surface area is covered by lava</u>.
- Moon has volcano <u>domes</u>.

Lecture

Main idea: Reasons why the volcano <u>explanation does not make sense</u>.
Key points:
- The craters are <u>perfect circles</u>.
- Volcanoes don't leave <u>a design like this</u>.
  - Now they think meteorites <u>left the craters</u>.
- The craters are older <u>than the volcanoes</u>.
  - The volcanoes formed <u>in the craters</u>

Page 73

Step 3

Topic: The reading and the lecture discuss theories on how the moon's craters were formed.

Answer Key

A. The reading says that volcanoes formed <u>the craters</u>.
  1. Hardened lava made <u>the craters</u>.
  2. The moon has lots of <u>volcano domes</u>.
B. The lecture says that volcanoes don't make <u>circles</u>.
  1. The craters were made by <u>meteorites</u>.
  2. The craters are older <u>than the volcanoes</u>.
  • The volcanoes were formed <u>in the craters</u>.
Conclusion: The lecture challenges the reading by showing how volcanoes could not have formed the craters on the moon.

Step 4

The reading and the lecture discuss <u>theories on how the craters on the moon were formed</u>.

The reading says that hardened lava from volcanoes was once thought to have formed <u>the craters</u>. The reading also says that people thought this because <u>the moon has lots of volcano domes</u>.

The lecture discusses why the volcano theory is not correct. In the lecture, the speaker says <u>volcanoes don't make perfect circles like craters, and therefore the craters were made by meteorites</u>. The speaker also says that the craters are older <u>than the volcanoes and that the volcanoes were actually formed in the craters</u>.

The lecture challenges the reading by <u>showing how volcanoes could not have formed the craters on the moon</u>.

Check-up

Page 74

1. principal	2. trap	3. useful
4. gravitational	5. hopefully	6. pulls

[Review 1]

Independent 1

Page 75

Sample Answer 1
Agree
Topic: Boys and girls <u>should</u> go to different schools.
A. <u>Teenagers are very self-conscious</u>.
  1. <u>They will be nervous more often</u>.
  2. <u>They will have more stress</u>.
B. <u>School is important for building friendships</u>.
  1. <u>My mother attended a girls' school and she still has the same friends</u>.
  2. <u>My dad attended a co-ed school and his friends are the guys he works with</u>.
Conclusion: Boys and girls should <u>go to different schools</u>.

I think that boys and girls should <u>go to different schools</u>. I think this because <u>many teenagers are very self-conscious</u>. I think that <u>if they have to mix with the opposite sex at school, they will be nervous more often. It might make students have more stress</u>. I also believe that <u>school is an important time to build good friendships</u>. For example, <u>my mother went to a girls' school. To this day, she is still good friends with the same girls. However, my dad attended a co-ed school. Nowadays, his closest friends are the guys he works with</u>. These are the reasons I think that <u>boys and girls should go to different schools</u>.

Sample Answer 2
Disagree
Topic: Boys and girls <u>should not</u> go to different schools.
A. <u>Boys and girls are equal</u>.
  1. <u>We can all achieve the same things</u>.
  2. <u>Separate schools convey a different message</u>.
B. <u>Mixed schools allow people to deal with relationships better</u>.
  1. <u>They can become friends easier</u>.
  2. <u>They may recognize their flaws earlier</u>.
Conclusion: Boys and girls should <u>attend the same schools</u>.

I think that boys and girls should <u>not go to different schools</u>. I think this because <u>we are told that boys and girls are equal</u>. I think that <u>we can achieve the same things in life. Separate schools convey a different message. It suggests that we have different educational needs</u>. I also believe that <u>mixed schools allow people to deal with relationships better</u>. For example, <u>boys and girls can become friends easier. Some kids' parents have bad relationships. Mixed schools may help them recognize flaws earlier. It may prevent them from imitating their parents' situation</u>. These are the reasons I think that <u>boys and girls should go to the same schools</u>.

Integrated 1

Page 76

Step 1

Reading

Main idea: Constellations are groups of <u>stars and have names</u>
Key points:
• It is hard to remember where <u>they all are</u>
• They will be found in the same place at the <u>same time of the year</u>
• They were given names describing what their <u>shapes looked like</u>

Lecture

Main idea: Constellations are helpful for remembering the stars

Key points:

- The stories are an explanation as to where these "pictures" came from
- These legends were useful to farmers
  - In some places, the seasons are very similar
  - Constellations appear at the same place each year
  - Farmers would know it was time for the harvest or other events
- This dependence on the sky became a part of cultures

Page 77

Step 3

Topic: The reading and the lecture are about why the constellations have names.

A. The reading discusses why they have names.
   1. The names help remember where the stars are.
   2. The names were descriptions of what they looked like.
B. The lecture discusses how constellations have stories.
C. The reading says that the constellations will be seen at the same place each year.
D. The speaker says some places have similar seasons.
   1. Farmers used constellations to decide when to have certain events like their harvest.
   2. Cultures are dependent on the sky.
Conclusion: The lecture supports the points made in the reading about why naming constellations was important.

Step 4

The reading and the lecture are about why constellations have names. The reading discusses that they have names to help remember where the stars were and that these names were descriptions of what they looked like. The lecture supports this by discussing how constellations have stories to further describe them. The reading also says that the constellations will be seen at the same place each year.

The speaker supports the reading by explaining how some places have similar seasons. Therefore, farmers used constellations to decide when to have certain events like their harvest. This was an example of how many cultures are dependent on the sky.

The lecture supports the points made in the reading about why naming constellations was important.

Integrated 2

Page 78

Step 1

Reading

Main idea: How World War II spread around the World
Key points:

- Fifty countries were involved
- Japan attacked US forces at Pearl Harbor
- US dropped atomic bombs on Hiroshima and Nagasaki
- There were huge social and economic effects

Lecture

Main idea: World War II is the most tragic war humanity has seen
Key points:

- The Holocaust was one of the most severe chapters
- Almost six million Jews were murdered
  - Nazis were responsible
- This was the most expensive war ever
  - Major cities had been badly bombed
  - Supplies of all kinds had been limited
- The situation took a long time to improve

Page 79

Step 3

Topic: The reading and the lecture are about the effects of World War II.

A. The reading discusses how it spread round the world.
   1. The Japanese attacked Pearl Harbor.
   2. The Americans dropped atomic bombs on Hiroshima and Nagasaki.
B. Other people also suffered social and economic effects.
C. The speaker says that WWII was a tragic war.
   1. The holocaust
   2. Almost six million Jews murdered by Nazis
D. WWII was expensive.
   1. Cities were bombed
   2. Supplies had been limited.
E. It took a long time to improve.
Conclusion: The lecture supports the points made in the reading by giving other social and economic effects of World War II.

Step 4

The reading and the lecture are about the effects of World War II. The reading discusses how it spread around the world and also affected the Japanese and Americans. The Japanese attacked Pearl Harbor and the Americans dropped atomic bombs on Hiroshima and Nagasaki. However, the reading says that other people also suffered social and economic effects.

Answer Key

The speaker supports this by saying that World War II was a tragic war and that in the holocaust almost six million Jews were murdered by Nazis. This was a social effect. The speaker also supports the reading by discussing the economic effects. World War II was the most expensive war ever because cities were bombed and supplies had been limited. It took a long time to improve.

The lecture supports the points made in the reading by giving other social and economic effects of World War II.

Independent 2

Page 80

Sample Answer 1
Disagree
Topic: Family is more important than friends.
A. Our parents helped us become who we are.
   1. I trust my family.
   2. I am more relaxed and honest with my family.
B. Our families love us regardless of our faults.
   1. If I become angry with my family, they know that I am just in a bad mood.
   2. Friends may not understand.
Conclusion: I think that family is more important.

I think that family is more important than friends. First, I think this because our parents helped us become who we are. Therefore, I trust my family. For example, I am more relaxed and honest with them than with my friends. Secondly, I think that our families love us regardless of our faults. For example, if I become angry with my family, they know that I am just in a bad mood. My friends may not understand. I appreciate my family for that. These are the reasons I think that family is more important.

Sample Answer 2
Agree
Topic: Friends are more important than family.
A. I do not have a close relationship with my family.
   1. My family hardly knows me.
   2. My friends know everything and I can say anything to them.
B. People cannot choose their family.
   1. I don't get along with my sister and I am made to feel guilty.
   2. I know that they are friends with me because they like me.
Conclusion: I think that friends are more important.

I think that friends are more important than family. First, I think this because I do not have a close relationship with my family. For example, my family hardly knows me. However, my friends know everything

about me. Also, I can say anything to my friends and I trust them. If I have a problem, I tell my friends. Secondly, people cannot choose their family. For example, when I don't get along with my sister, I am made to feel guilty. However, my friends have the right not to be my friend. I know that they are friends with me because they like me. These are the reasons I think that friends are more important.

[Unit 7]

Independent

Getting Ready

Page 81

B
1. The reason was my sister felt lonely.
2. I felt sorry for her.
3. Others in my family said I should play with her.
4. I think that she felt better when I played with her.

Practice

Page 82

B
(A) Agree

C
Topic: Parents should not cry in front of their children.
A. It scares kids.
   1. They want their parents to protect them.
   2. They will be frightened.
   3. They will think something terrible happened.
B. Kids should not know about bad problems.
   1. Parents cry because of a crisis like losing a job.
   2. Kids cannot understand these things.
Conclusion: Instead, parents should go to a counselor or cry in private.

D
First of all
Second
Therefore

Page 83

E
(B) Disagree

F
Topic: Parents should cry in front of their children.
A. It's healthy for parents to express their emotions.
   1. Parents will feel better.
   2. Kids will see that it is all right to cry sometimes.
B. Parents and kids can feel closer.
   1. Kids can comfort their parents.
   2. Kids and parents can talk about their problems together.

Conclusion: I think <u>parents should cry in front of their children and not feel bad about it</u>.

G

First

Second

So

H

1. private   2. counselor   3. emotion
4. trust   5. crisis

Test

Page 84

Sample answer 1

Agree

Topic: I think that parents <u>should not</u> cry in front of their children.

A. <u>Children can become frightened</u>.
    1. <u>My parents had a big fight and my mom started crying</u>.
    2. <u>My sister ran into the bedroom, and it was hard to comfort her</u>.
B. <u>Children cannot do anything about a big crisis</u>.
    1. <u>My friend's mom cried when she lost her job</u>.
    2. <u>My friend felt bad and did not know what to do</u>.
Conclusion: I feel parents <u>should not</u> cry in front of their children.

I think that parents <u>should not</u> cry in front of their children. I think this because <u>the children can become frightened</u>. For example, <u>one day my parents had a big fight. My mom started crying in front of my sister and me. We got very scared. My sister ran into the bedroom, and it was hard to comfort her</u>. I also believe this because <u>kids cannot do anything about a big crisis</u>. For example, <u>my friend's mom cried when she lost her job. It just made my friend feel bad. He did not know what to do</u>. This is why I feel parents <u>should not</u> cry in front of their children.

Sample Answer 2

Disagree

Topic: I think that parents <u>should</u> cry in front of their children.

A. <u>People should share their emotions</u>.
    1. <u>My parents both cried when my grandma died</u>.
    2. <u>We felt better after we cried</u>.
B. <u>Kids can sometimes help parents feel better</u>.
    1. <u>My mom was upset because no one helps her clean the house</u>.
    2. <u>We said we were sorry and we helped her clean</u>.
Conclusion: I feel parents <u>can</u> cry in front of their children.

I think that parents <u>should</u> cry in front of their kids. I think this because <u>people should share their emotions</u>. For example, <u>my parents both cried when my grandma died. It made me cry too. However, we felt better after we cried</u>. I also believe this because <u>kids can sometimes help parents feel better</u>. For example, <u>my mom started crying one day. We asked her what was wrong. She said she was too tired. She was upset because no one helps her clean the house. So we said we were sorry and we helped her clean</u>. This is why I feel parents <u>can</u> cry in front of their children. <u>It is a natural thing</u>.

Integrated

Getting Ready

Page 85

B

1. B
2. They might talk about a famous autobiography, why people like autobiographies, or why authors want to write about their feelings.

Practice

Page 86

A

(B)

B

Reading

Main idea: Autobiographies are books people write about <u>their own lives</u>.

Key points:

• We can understand the author's <u>feelings</u>
• Autobiographies also teach us about <u>problems</u>
• Autobiographies inspire us to <u>make things better</u>

Lecture

Main idea: Frederick Douglass wrote an autobiography that helped <u>end slavery in the United States</u>

Key points:

• He was a slave, but he <u>escaped</u>
• The autobiography helped raise people's <u>awareness about slavery</u>
• The autobiography also <u>gave other slaves courage to speak out</u>

Page 87

D

The reading explains what an autobiography is and why this genre is important. One reason is that people are <u>inspired by</u> the author's courage. Another reason is that these books teach us about problems.

Answer Key

The lecture illustrates how an autobiography <u>helped end slavery</u> in the United States. The speaker says that Frederick Douglass wrote his autobiography after he <u>escaped from slavery</u>. The speaker says that many people read his book and it made them think about slavery. The speaker also explains that it gave other <u>slaves courage</u>. They began to speak out about their problems.

E

1. admire   2. awareness   3. author
4. courage   5. genre

Test

Page 88

Step 1

Reading

Main idea: A memoir is a book about a time <u>in a person's life</u>.

Key points:
- It is about a certain time in a person's life, not <u>their whole life</u>
- It is usually about a major event the person <u>lived through</u>
- It talks about a <u>part of history</u>

Lecture

Main idea: Anne Frank wrote a famous memoir about <u>World War II</u>.

Key points:
- Her family had to hide and she wrote <u>about it</u>
- It tells about the terrible things <u>that happened</u>
- Many people think she was very wise and they admire <u>her for her courage</u>
- Many people learn about <u>World War II</u>

Page 89

Step 3

Topic: The reading and the lecture are about how a memoir can help people learn about history.
A. The reading says memoirs are <u>books</u>.
   1. They are about a certain <u>time</u>.
   2. They usually focus on a major <u>event a person lived through</u>.
B. The lecture discusses a famous memoir that Anne <u>Frank wrote</u>.
   1. Her family was in hiding during <u>World War II</u>.
   2. She told about the terrible things that <u>happened during the war</u>.
   3. People think she is wise and <u>admire her for her courage</u>.
   4. It also teaches <u>about World War II</u>.
Conclusion: The lecture supports the points made in the reading about memoirs by giving a famous example of a memoir from World War II.

Step 4

The reading and the lecture are <u>about how a memoir can help people learn about history</u>. The reading says that memoirs <u>are books in which the author describes a certain time in his or her life</u>. The reading also says that memoirs usually focus on <u>a major event</u>.

The lecture then discusses a famous memoir Anne Frank wrote when <u>her family was in hiding during World War II</u>. In the lecture, the speaker explains that Anne Frank told about <u>the terrible things that happened during the war</u>. People think she is <u>wise and admire her for her courage</u>. It also teaches about <u>World War II</u>.

The lecture supports the <u>points made in the reading about memoirs by giving a famous example of a memoir from World War II</u>.

Check-up

Page 90

1. terrible   2. wise   3. frightened
4. comfort   5. speak out   6. natural

[Unit 8]

Independent

Getting Ready

Page 91

B

1. It was <u>when our class volunteered to help at the nursing home</u>.
2. I did this because <u>my teacher said I had to</u>.
3. I felt <u>that I did not want to go at first, but I liked talking to the old men, because they were funny</u>.
4. I think that <u>the older people really enjoyed talking with us</u>.

Practice

Page 92

B

(B) Disagree

C

Topic: Young people <u>have more</u> fun than old people.
A. Young people look for <u>adventure</u>.
   1. Young people like to solve <u>mysteries and learn new things</u>.
   2. Old people just want to <u>relax and talk</u>.
B. Young people <u>laugh more</u>.
   1. Young people are more <u>amused with things</u>.
   2. Old people have <u>seen it all</u>.
Conclusion: I believe <u>old people don't want to bother with fun</u>.

D
First
Second

Page 93

E
(A) Agree

F
Topic: Older people <u>have more</u> fun than younger people.
A. Grandmother is more <u>fun than my friends</u>.
   1. She tells <u>jokes and makes people laugh</u>.
   2. She is <u>retired and takes many trips</u>.
B. Older people tell <u>good stories</u>.
   1. They have <u>lived a long time and have learned so many things</u>.
   2. They can tell you about exciting <u>adventures</u>.
Conclusion: I cannot wait to be <u>older and have more fun</u>.

G
Also
For these reasons

H
1. throughout   2. abundant   3. amuse
4. bother   5. retire

Test

Page 94

Sample Answer 1
Agree
Topic: I think that <u>older people</u> have more fun than <u>younger people</u>.
A. <u>I have spent a lot of time around old people</u>.
   1. <u>My grandmother is retired and lives in a home with other old people</u>.
   2. <u>They are always laughing</u>.
B. <u>Old people are always doing things</u>.
   1. <u>They play fun, relaxing games like bingo and cards</u>.
   2. <u>They sing and go shopping</u>.
Conclusion: I think that <u>older people</u> have more fun.

   I think that <u>older people</u> have more fun than <u>younger people</u>. This is because <u>I have spent a lot of time around old people</u>. For instance, <u>my grandmother is retired and lives in a home with many other old people. They are always laughing</u>, so I think that they have more fun. I think that the <u>old people there are always doing things</u>. For example, <u>they like playing fun, relaxing games like bingo and cards. They sing sometimes. They go out on shopping trips too. They laugh a lot</u>. For these reasons, I think that <u>old people have more fun</u>.

Sample Answer 2
Disagree
Topic: I think that <u>younger people</u> have more fun than <u>older people</u>.
A. <u>I have so much fun with my friends</u>.
   1. <u>We find everything amusing</u>.
   2. <u>We have an abundance of fun</u>.
B. <u>Older people sometimes don't have many friends</u>.
   1. <u>My grandmother just stays home alone and does not see her friends anymore</u>.
   2. <u>Young people have many friends to do active things with</u>.
Conclusion: I think that <u>younger people</u> have more fun.

   I think that <u>younger people</u> have more fun than <u>older people</u>. This is because <u>I have so much fun with my friends</u>. For instance, <u>we find everything amusing. We have an abundance of fun every time we are together</u>. I think that <u>older people sometimes don't have many friends to do things with</u>. For example, <u>my grandmother just stays home alone and sits down the whole day. She does not see her friends anymore. I feel bad for her. I feel young people have many friends to do active things with. We ride skateboards and go swimming in the summer</u>. For these reasons, I think that <u>young people have more fun than older people</u>.

Integrated

Getting Ready

Page 95

B
1. A
2. They might talk about how we make CO_2, how much CO_2 humans make, or how volcanoes create CO_2.

Practice

Page 96

A
(B)

B

Reading

Main idea: CO_2 that causes global warming comes from <u>two natural sources</u>.

Key points:
• Volcanoes put 255 million <u>tons into the air annually</u>
• Forest fires in Indonesia <u>released 23 billion tons in 1997 and 1998</u>

Answer Key

Lecture

Main idea: Man-made CO_2 is <u>the real problem</u>.
Key points:
- Cars create a lot of <u>CO_2</u>
  - US drivers released 314 million tons of <u>CO_2 in 2004</u>
- Power plants <u>are a huge source of CO_2</u>
  - CO_2 from <u>one forest fire is tiny compared to that from power plants</u>
  - Plants in the US give off 1.5 billion tons <u>annually</u>

Page 97

D

The reading explains how CO_2 is harmful. It explains that <u>two natural ways</u> that CO_2 is released into the air is through volcanoes and forest fires.

The lecture talks about how nature was not the <u>biggest problem</u>. The lecture discusses how driving cars and using <u>power plants</u> releases much more carbon than nature does. The speaker says that US cars released 314 million tons of CO_2 into the air in 2004. The amount of CO_2 that humans make with cars and power plants is <u>much more</u> than volcanoes and fires.

The lecture challenges the reading by showing how man-made CO_2 is worse than natural-made CO_2.

E

1. produces   2. vehicles   3. tons
4. create   5. annually

Test

Page 98

Step 1

Reading

Main idea: Cows create methane gas, which <u>causes pollution</u>.
Key points:
- Cows <u>burp methane gas into the air</u>
- Cow waste releases gas and <u>pollutes water sources</u>

Lecture

Main idea: Cows are not causing a lot <u>of pollution</u>.
Key points:
- Methane gas that cows produce can be <u>reduced</u>
- A natural chemical reduces the methane in their <u>burps by seventy percent</u>
- Cow waste does not give off <u>much methane gas</u>
- Cow waste is <u>natural</u>

Page 99

Step 3

Topic: The reading and the lecture discuss how cows release methane gas and cause pollution.
A. The reading says that
  1. cows create a lot of methane gas by <u>burping</u>
  2. water is polluted by <u>cows' waste</u>
B. The lecture says that
  1. cows are not causing <u>a lot of pollution</u>
  2. cow burping has already been reduced by 70% using a <u>natural chemical</u>
  3. cow waste is natural and does not give off <u>much methane gas</u>
Conclusion; The lecture challenges the reading by arguing that cows do not cause that much pollution.

Step 4

The reading and the lecture <u>discuss how cows release methane gas and cause pollution</u>. The reading says that cows create a lot of <u>methane gas by burping</u>. It also says that water is <u>polluted by their waste</u>.

In the lecture, the speaker challenges the reading by saying that cows are not <u>causing a lot of pollution</u>. The speaker says that waste from cows' burping has already been reduced by <u>70% using a natural chemical</u>. The speaker also says that cow waste is <u>natural and does not give off much methane gas</u>.

The lecture challenges the reading by <u>arguing that cows do not cause much pollution from the methane gas they release</u>.

Check-up

Page 100

1. mystery   2. giggle   3. rises
4. barrier   5. power plants   6. adventure

[Unit 9]

Independent

Getting Ready

Page 101

B

1. The activity was <u>going to an amusement park</u>.
2. I chose this activity because <u>I like to ride roller coasters</u>.
3. I could <u>not have done this activity without money</u>.
4. I could have <u>gone to the park and played baseball with my friends</u>.

Practice

Page 102

B

(A) Agree

C

Topic: People are <u>happier</u> when they have more money.
A. You don't need to <u>worry about paying your bills</u>.
   1. People who don't have money often <u>have to borrow</u>.
   2. Debt can cause <u>anxiety and you cannot be happy</u>.
B. You can buy <u>what you need</u>.
   1. My mom and dad <u>are happy</u>.
   2. People <u>worry and argue less</u>.
Conclusion: This is why I believe <u>people are happier when they have money</u>.

D

First
Second

Page 103

E

(B) Disagree

F

Topic: I <u>don't think</u> people are happier if they have more money.
A. Some people with big incomes are <u>unhappy</u>.
   1. Paul's dad is rich, but his family is <u>not happy</u>.
   2. My family is happy, but we <u>don't have as much money</u>.
B. Money can make people <u>worry</u>.
   1. Some people <u>want too much money</u>.
   2. Paul's dad wants too much money, and it makes his <u>family argue</u>.
Conclusion: People are happier when <u>they don't want to have a lot of money</u>.

G

To begin
Also
Therefore

H

1. income	2. anxiety	3. steady
4. debt	5. owe	

Test

Page 104

Sample Answer 1
Agree

Topic: I <u>think people are happier</u> when they have more money.
A. <u>Money helps people do what they want</u>.
   1. <u>My family has a steady income and we like to go on vacation</u>.
   2. <u>We can pay to go where we want and it makes us happy</u>.
B. <u>Money helps people live without worry</u>.
   1. <u>Some people live in debt because they buy things they can't afford</u>.
   2. <u>James's family borrows lots of money and his mom and dad always argue</u>.
Conclusion: A person <u>cannot</u> be happy without money.

   I <u>think people are happier</u> when they have more money. First, I think <u>money helps people do what they want. You can pay for things you want to do</u>. For example, <u>my family has a steady income and we like to go on vacation. We can pay to go where we want. It is really fun. It makes our family happy</u>. Second, I think <u>money helps people live without worry</u>. For instance, <u>some people live in debt. They buy things they can't afford. My friend James's family borrows lots of money. His mom and dad always argue about how much they owe</u>. I think a person <u>cannot</u> be happy without money.

Sample Answer 2
Disagree
Topic: I <u>don't think people are happier</u> when they have more money.
A. <u>Money can't buy happiness</u>.
   1. <u>My family is rich, but we aren't always happy</u>.
   2. <u>We also have a lot of anxiety about other things</u>.
B. <u>Being able to buy lots of stuff does not make someone happy</u>.
   1. <u>Some people think that having more things makes them happy</u>.
   2. <u>I am happy when my dad is nice to me and spends time with me</u>.
Conclusion: A person <u>can</u> be happy without money.

   I <u>don't think people are happier</u> when they have more money. First, I think <u>money can't buy happiness</u>. For example, <u>my family is rich, but we aren't always happy. We are happy sometimes, but we also have a lot of anxiety about other things like my grades and our health</u>. Second, I think <u>being able to buy lots of stuff does not make someone happy</u>. For instance, <u>some people think that having more things makes them happy. I am happy when my dad is nice to me. I want him to spend time with me. I don't want him to give me things</u>. I think a person <u>can</u> be happy without money.

Answer Key

Getting Ready

Page 105

B

1. B
2. They might talk about the different categories, what the pyramid looks like, or how much is suggested to eat.

Practice

Page 106

A

(A)

B

Reading

Main idea: The food pyramid teaches people about healthy eating.
Key points:
- The government decided on the pyramid shape
- The pyramid separates food categories into different levels and sections

Lecture

Main idea: What each level of the food pyramid is
Key points:
- The large bottom of the pyramid means you should eat bread, cereal, and pasta
- Only two to five servings of fruits and vegetables
- The top level of the pyramid shows to eat very little sugar and fats

Page 107

D

The reading explains what the food pyramid is and how it teaches people how to eat healthy. The pyramid suggests a certain amount of foods to eat from different categories.

The lecture explains the categories in depth. The speaker says that the bottom group is for breads cereals, and pasta. People should eat a lot of these. The speaker also says that the top group contains sweets and fats. People should eat very little food from this group.

E

1. section   2. diagram   3. government
4. refer   5. category

Test

Page 108

Step 1

Reading

Main idea: The old food pyramid was replaced with a new system.
Key points:
- Americans were gaining weight
- The old pyramid was the problem
- Research showed that different people need different amounts of food

Lecture

Main idea: How the new system is different
Key points:
- There are now twelve different pyramids
- The food categories are now not divided by levels but are side by side
- The government has a website
  - People can find their personal pyramids

Page 109

Step 3

Topic: The reading and the lecture are about the new food pyramids.
A. The reading says that the new pyramids were developed because Americans were gaining weight.
  1. They thought the old pyramid was the problem.
  2. People need different amounts of food.
B. The lecture says that there are now 12 pyramids.
  1. Each person can find his or her personal pyramid.
  2. Food categories are now side by side and not divided by levels.
Conclusion: The lecture supports the reading because it gives examples of how the new pyramids are different from the old one.

Step 4

The reading and the lecture are about the new food pyramids. The reading says that the new pyramids are because Americans were gaining weight. They thought the old pyramid was the problem. The reading also says that research showed that different people need different amounts of food.

The lecture supports this by explaining that there are now twelve pyramids. Each person can find his or her personal pyramid. In the lecture, the speaker also says that the food categories are now side by side, and not divided by levels.

The lecture supports the reading because it gives examples of how the new pyramid is different from the old one.

Page 110

1. bill
2. borrow
3. finally
4. argue
5. serving
6. level

[Unit 10]

Independent

Getting Ready

Page 111

B

1. It was when I cut my hair like Julia Roberts.
2. I did this because I think she is very pretty.
3. I felt happy because I looked better with my hair like hers.
4. I think that it was a good idea because I like my hair better this way.

Practice

Page 112

B

(A) Agree

C

Topic: People care too much about what celebrities do.
A. Celebrities are in the news all the time.
   1. News does not show what is going on in the world.
   2. News seems to think everyone wants to see everything celebrities do.
B. TV shows devoted to celebrity gossip.
   1. Celebrities are just people.
   2. TV shows talk about every detail of their lives.
Conclusion: I think others care too much.

D

Also
But
However

Page 113

E

(B) Disagree

F

Topic: People should care about what celebrities do.
A. They can be good role models.
   1. They do things to help the needy and the environment.
   2. They set good examples.

B. They start trends in our culture.
   1. We need to know what they wear, eat, or where they shop.
   2. This is how popular trends that are important to kids start.
Conclusion: Knowing what celebrities do is important.

G

First
For example
The second reason

H

1. Personal
2. devoted
3. affairs
4. trends
5. annoy

Test

Page 114

Sample Answer 1
Agree
Topic: People care too much about what celebrities do.
A. I get annoyed at how much gossip there is.
   1. I see their pictures and stories about them everywhere.
   2. No matter what they are doing, people are taking their pictures.
B. There are more important things and people to photograph.
   1. I am devoted to reading about people who are doing good things in the world.
   2. I am tired of seeing celebrities who have lots of problems get so much attention.
Conclusion: I think that people care too much about what celebrities do.

I think that people care too much about what celebrities do. This is because I get annoyed at how much gossip there is about them. I think that because I see their pictures and stories about them everywhere. No matter what they are doing, people are taking their pictures. I feel that there are more important things and people to photograph. For example, I am devoted to reading about people who are doing good things in the world. I am tired of seeing celebrities who have lots of problems get so much attention. For these reasons, I think that people care too much about what celebrities do.

Sample Answer 2
Disagree
Topic: People should care about what celebrities do.
A. It is fun to know what famous people are doing all the time.

Answer Key

1. I like to know where my favorite celebrity shops.
2. I like to follow the same trends as my favorite celebrities.
B. It is okay for us to hear about and see what celebrities do.
   1. They probably do not mind too much.
   2. I would be happy that I was so famous.
Conclusion: I think it is good for people to care about what celebrities do.

I think that people should care about what celebrities do. This is because I think it is fun to know what famous people are doing all the time. I think that because I like to know where my favorite celebrity shops. I like to follow the same trends as my favorite celebrities. They are my role models. I feel that it is OK for us to hear about and see what celebrities do. For example, they probably do not mind too much. If it were me, I would be happy that I was so famous. For these reasons, I think it is good for people to care about what celebrities do.

Integrated

Getting Ready
Page 115

B
1. A
2. They might talk about why spy chips are helpful, if people like them, or other ways the chips are used.

Practice
Page 116

A
(A)

B
Reading
Main idea: Radio frequency ID tags are helpful to businesses
Key points:
- They are also called spy chips
- The tags help owners track new shipments
- The tags help cut down on theft

Lecture
Main idea: People think spy chips are not good
Key points:
- Companies track customers, not shipments
  - They get personal information
- Chips could be a health risk
  - They emit electromagnetic energy

Page 117

D

The reading explains how radio frequency ID tags help businesses. These chips are put into products and can be tracked almost anywhere.

The lecture argues that people do not think this is a good idea. The speaker talks about companies being able to track their customers. People think their personal information should be private. The speaker also says that the chips might be a health risk. The tags emit electromagnetic energy that might not be safe. People have stopped buying things with tags for these reasons.

E
1. theft   2. track   3. device
4. signal   5. shipment

Test
Page 118
Step 1
Reading
Main idea: Technology can help parents keep teens safe
Key points:
- Devices in cell phones tell parents where their child is
- Chips in cars tell parents where and how fast the teen is driving

Lecture
Main idea: Technology does not really make kids safer
Key points:
- Chips only track phones, not kids
- Chips in cars only give parents information
  - They can't protect teens from accidents

Page 119
Step 3
Topic: The reading and the lecture discuss new technology parents can use.
A. The reading says that devices can be placed in a teenager's cell phone or car.
   1. These devices track them.
   2. The devices check where they are and how fast they are driving.
B. The lecture states that the chip may not make kids safer.
   1. The phone can be tracked but not the teen.
   2. The chip cannot protect a teen from being in an accident.
Conclusion: The lecture challenges the reading, because it argues that the chips do not make teens any safer.

Step 4

The reading and the lecture <u>discuss new technology parents can use</u>.

The reading says that <u>devices can be placed in a teenager's cell phone or car</u>. These devices help keep teens safe by <u>tracking them and checking where they are and how fast they are driving</u>.

However, the lecture states that the chip may not <u>make kids any safer</u>. The speaker says that the phone can <u>be tracked but not the teen. The speaker also says that the chip cannot protect a teen from being in an accident</u>.

The lecture challenges the reading because <u>it argues that the chips do not make teens any safer</u>.

Check-up

Page 120

1. celebrity
2. spy
3. chip
4. gossip
5. tag
6. role models

[Unit 11]

Independent

Getting Ready

Page 121

1. The game was <u>somewhat violent because it had guns but it looked like a cartoon</u>.
2. The game <u>made us hit people, but it didn't give points for doing it</u>.
3. I think this game would <u>make people feel excited</u>.
4. I think that this game was <u>not much like real life at all</u>.

Practice

Page 122

B

(B) Disagree

C

Topic: Video games with guns <u>do not make</u> people violent.
A. Video games are <u>not real</u>.
  1. Video games do not replicate <u>real life</u>.
  2. It does not mean I will <u>behave violently</u>.
B. Not everyone that plays video games is <u>violent</u>.
  1. Criminals existed <u>before video games</u>.
  2. I know right <u>from wrong</u>.
Conclusion: I do not think that <u>video games make people violent</u>.

D

First
However
Second
Therefore

Page 123

E

(A) Agree

F

Topic: Video games <u>make people</u> more violent.
A. People used to be <u>more peaceful</u>.
  1. Video games encourage <u>people to act like criminals</u>.
  2. A young boy stabbed someone and said <u>a video game gave him the idea</u>.
B. The challenge in many <u>video games is to hurt people</u>.
  1. This teaches that it is <u>good to hurt people</u>.
  2. Points are awarded for <u>hurting people</u>.
Conclusion: These games teach people to <u>behave violently</u>.

G

First
Now
Then
Second

H

1. actually
2. award
3. behave
4. criminal
5. replicate

Test

Page 124

Sample Answer 1

Agree

Topic: I <u>think</u> video games that have fighting or guns make people more violent.
A. <u>Video games teach people how to hurt others</u>.
  1. <u>You have to shoot people when you play</u>.
  2. <u>It teaches how to use a gun</u>.
B. <u>Video games say it is OK to hurt people</u>.
  1. <u>Some games make you hurt people to get to the next level</u>.
  2. <u>It suggests that hurting people is good and that it is OK to be a criminal</u>.
Conclusion: I think video games <u>teach people to behave violently</u>.

Answer Key

I <u>think</u> video games that have fighting or guns make people more violent. To begin, I think video games <u>teach people how to hurt others</u>. Some video games <u>have guns. You have to shoot people when you play. This teaches how to use a gun. I played a game where I had to aim and press a button. Then the gun fired.</u> Second, <u>I think games say it is OK to hurt people</u>. I think this because <u>some games make you hurt people to get to the next level. You are awarded points for hurting someone. This suggests that hurting people is good and that it is ok to be a criminal.</u> This is why I think video games <u>teach people to behave violently</u>.

Sample Answer 2

Disagree

Topic: I <u>don't think</u> video games that have fighting or guns make people more violent.
A. <u>Video games are just fun</u>.
  1. <u>Playing video games is just like watching a movie or TV show</u>.
  2. <u>People play video games just to be entertained</u>.
B. <u>My friends and I have played violent video games for years, but we are not violent</u>.
  1. <u>We play video games to have fun and challenge ourselves</u>.
  2. <u>We do not replicate the violence</u>.
Conclusion: I think video games <u>are not a cause of violence</u>.

I <u>don't think</u> video games that have fighting or guns make people more violent. To begin, I think video games <u>are just fun</u>. Some video games <u>are just like watching a movie or TV show with violence. People play video games just to be entertained</u>. Second, <u>my friends and I have played violent video games for years, but we are not violent</u>. I think this because <u>none of us has ever gotten into a fight. We play video games to have fun and challenge ourselves. However, we do not replicate the violence. If video games made people violent then we would hurt each other all the time</u>. This is why I think video games <u>are not a cause of violence</u>.

Integrated

Getting Ready

Page 125

B
1. B
2. They might talk about where the continental glaciers are, how continental glaciers form, or other ways that continental glaciers differ from other glaciers.

Practice

Page 126

A

(A)

B

Reading

Main idea: Continental glaciers are different from <u>other glaciers in two ways</u>
Key points:
• Continental glaciers are very <u>large</u>
• Continental glaciers can change the <u>landscape in bigger ways</u>

Lecture

Main idea: The scale and power of continental <u>glaciers</u>
Key points:
• One sheet of ice covers <u>eighty-five percent of Greenland</u>
  - It is three meters <u>thick at some points</u>
• If Antarctica glaciers melted, oceans would <u>rise by sixty meters</u>
• Over time, glaciers can change the <u>face of the Earth</u>

Page 127

D

The reading explains what a continental glacier is and the two ways that they differ from other glaciers. These glaciers are <u>very large</u> and hold eighty percent of the planet's fresh water. They also have the power to <u>change the shape</u> of the Earth by making valleys or wearing away mountain peaks.

The lecture explains the scale of these glaciers. The speaker says that a Greenland glacier is three kilometers thick <u>at some points</u>. The speaker <u>also points out</u> that continental glacier bottoms wear away at the Earth. Over time, they can change what the Earth looks like.

E
1. ecological   2. fascinating   3. glacier
4. differ   5. landscape

Test

Page 128

Step 1

Reading

Main idea: The glaciers on Earth are <u>becoming smaller</u>.
Key points:
• Global warming is changing <u>the Earth's climate</u>
• The loss of forests near mountain glaciers <u>causes melting</u>

Lecture

Main idea: Two of the world's glaciers are <u>disappearing</u>.
Key points:
• The largest glacier in North America is <u>disappearing</u>
• The glacier on Mount Kilimanjaro is <u>melting</u>
  - Farmers have <u>cut or burnt away the trees</u>

Page 129

Step 3

Topic: The reading and the lecture are about how the world's glaciers are disappearing.
A. The reading discusses two reasons for <u>glaciers becoming smaller</u>.
  1. Global warming is <u>changing the Earth's climate</u>.
  2. The loss of forests near <u>mountain glaciers causes them to melt</u>.
B. The lecture gives examples of how this is affecting <u>two of the world's glaciers</u>.
  1. The largest glacier in North America is <u>disappearing because of global warming</u>.
  2. The loss of trees is making Mount Kilimanjaro's <u>glacier melt away</u>.
    • Farmers have <u>cut and burnt them</u>.
Conclusion: The lecture supports the points made in the reading, because it gives examples of glaciers melting from global warming and the loss of trees.

Step 4

The reading and the lecture are about <u>how the world's glaciers are disappearing</u>. The reading discusses <u>two reasons for glaciers becoming smaller</u>. One reason is because <u>global warming is changing the Earth's climate</u> and the other reason is <u>the loss of forests near mountain glaciers causes them to melt</u>.

The lecture gives examples of <u>how this is affecting two of the world's glaciers</u>. The speaker talks about how the largest <u>glacier in North America is disappearing because of global warming</u>. The speaker also discusses how the loss of <u>trees, because farmers have cut and burnt them, is making Mount Kilimanjaro's glacier melt away</u>.

The lecture supports the points made in the reading, because <u>it gives examples of glaciers melting from global warming and the loss of trees</u>.

Check-up

Page 130

1. peaceful   2. wear away   3. fresh
4. stab   5. shoot   6. sheet

[Unit 12]

Independent

Getting Ready
Page 131
B
1. This person is <u>my grandmother</u>.
2. He/she does because <u>she grew up in Mexico and moved to the US after she got married</u>.
3. Some benefits of speaking another language are <u>being able to talk to more people and understand things that others cannot</u>.
4. Someone might want to learn to speak another language because <u>it might be interesting or it might help him or her get a better job</u>.

Practice
Page 132
B
(A) Agree

C
Topic: Students <u>should</u> learn a foreign language in school.
A. Helps get into <u>college</u>.
  1. Most colleges require students to have <u>studied a foreign language</u>.
  2. Some only <u>accept students who have taken two years of foreign language courses</u>.
B. Helps get a higher paying <u>job</u>.
  1. Businesses think bilingual people are an <u>asset</u>.
  2. People who <u>can translate make good incomes</u>.
Conclusion: I believe <u>it is good to learn another language</u>.

D
First
A second benefit
Therefore

Page 133
E
(B) Disagree

F
Topic: I <u>do not think</u> that all students should learn a foreign language in school.
A. Students already have too much <u>to learn</u>.
  1. They have many subjects and <u>time is scarce</u>.
  2. A different <u>language would be difficult</u>.
B. Students already learned their <u>native language</u>.
  1. They live in a country that <u>speaks that language</u>.
  2. They already have what they need to <u>talk and work with other people</u>.

Conclusion: I think <u>students should spend time learning other things</u>.

G

First of all
The second reason

H

1. foreign   2. requires   3. scarce
4. asset   5. native

Test

Page 134

Sample Answer 1

Agree

Topic: I think students <u>should</u> learn a foreign language in school.
A. <u>It may be an asset when they get into college</u>.
   1. <u>Bilingual people are smarter</u>.
   2. <u>Bilingual people are scarce and get good jobs</u>.
B. <u>I would like to learn a foreign language</u>.
   1. <u>I can go to visit other places</u>.
   2. <u>It would be fun to go to France and speak French</u>.
Conclusion: <u>I feel like it is a good idea for students</u> to learn another language in school.

I think students <u>should have to</u> learn a foreign language in school. This is because <u>it may be an asset when they get into college</u>. For example, <u>my brother is taking Spanish. He says it makes you smarter to be bilingual. Bilingual people are also scarce, so they get good jobs</u>. I think that <u>I would like to learn a foreign language, so that I can go visit other places when I am older. I feel like it would be fun to go to France and speak French</u>. For these reasons, I <u>feel like it is a good idea for students to learn another language in school</u>.

Sample Answer 2

Disagree

Topic: I think students <u>should not have to</u> learn a foreign language in school.
A. <u>Not everyone wants to be bilingual</u>.
   1. <u>Some people have trouble in their native language</u>.
   2. <u>It is not fair to require a student to learn another language</u>.
B. <u>Students should get to choose what they want to do</u>.
   1. <u>I want to be a kindergarten teacher</u>.
   2. <u>I do not need to know another language</u>.
Conclusion: <u>I do not think students should have</u> to learn another language in school.

I think students <u>should not have to</u> learn a foreign language in school. This is because <u>not everyone wants to be bilingual</u>. For example, <u>some people have trouble in their native language already. I think that it is not fair to require a student to learn another language, when he or she is not good at their native one</u>. I think that <u>students should get to choose what they want to do. I want to be a kindergarten teacher. I do not need to know another language. I will be teaching in English</u>. For these reasons, I <u>do not think students should have to learn another language in school</u>.

Integrated

Getting Ready

Page 135

B

1. A
2. They might talk about the kinds of music that made up Rock 'n' Roll, who really started Rock 'n' Roll, or who else helped Elvis make Rock 'n' Roll popular.

Practice

Page 136

A

(A)

B

Reading

Main idea: Elvis started <u>Rock 'n' Roll</u>.
Key points:
• A famous magazine said Elvis <u>introduced Rock 'n' Roll in 1954</u>
• This was the first time music had <u>a mass appeal across America</u>
  - Elvis performed in front <u>of thousands of fans</u>

Lecture

Main idea: Elvis didn't truly start <u>Rock 'n' Roll</u>
Key points:
• One of most popular hits was recorded before <u>Elvis's first record</u>
  - *Rock Around the Clock* by Bill Haley and <u>the Comets in 1955</u>
• Radio DJ called Alan Freed came up with the <u>name for Rock 'n' Roll three years before Elvis's first record</u>
  - He also produced the first <u>Rock 'n' Roll concerts</u>

D

The reading explains the beginnings of Rock 'n' Roll. Many believe that Elvis Presley introduced Rock 'n' Roll. This is because he had a <u>mass appeal</u> and performed in front of thousands of fans.

The lecture claims that Rock 'n' Roll did not begin with Elvis. The speaker credits <u>Bill Haley and the Comets</u> with the first Rock 'n' Roll hit. The song was called *Rock Around the Clock*. This song was recorded before Elvis's first record. The lecture also states that <u>Alan Freed</u>, a radio DJ, introduced Rock 'n' Roll to audiences in 1951. This was <u>three years before</u> Elvis produced his first record.

E

1. phenomenon   2. audience   3. appeal
4. perform   5. icon

Test

Page 138

Step 1

Reading

Main idea: Rock 'n' Roll music has <u>strong ties to blues music</u>.
Key points:
• Used the same <u>instruments as the new blues</u>
• R and B artists became <u>icons in America</u>
  - Little Richard and Chuck Berry prepared audiences for Rock 'n' Roll

Lecture

Main idea: Rock 'n' Roll really came from <u>rockabilly music</u>.
Key points:
• Rockabilly music is <u>fast-paced country rock music</u>.
• Rockabilly musicians were <u>early icons of Rock 'n' Roll</u>.
  - Wanda Jackson was <u>famous</u>

Page 139

Step 3

Topic: The reading and the lecture are about where Rock 'n' Roll came from.
A. The reading says that
  1. Rock 'n' Roll has strong ties <u>to blues music</u>
  2. R and B artists prepared <u>audiences for Rock 'n' Roll</u>
     • Little <u>Richard</u>
     • Chuck <u>Berry</u>
B. The lecture explains that Rock 'n' Roll <u>may have come from rockabilly music</u>.
  1. Like country music <u>with a faster pace</u>
  2. Rockabilly artists, like Wanda Jackson, were <u>the early icons</u>

Conclusion: The lecture challenges the reading by saying Rock 'n' Roll music came from rockabilly music, not the blues.

Step 4

The reading and the lecture <u>are about where Rock 'n' Roll came from</u>. The reading says that Rock 'n' Roll has <u>strong ties to blues music</u>. The reading also says that R and B <u>artists like Little Richard and Chuck Berry prepared audiences for Rock 'n' Roll</u>.

The lecture explains that Rock 'n' Roll <u>may have come from rockabilly music</u>. The speaker says that rockabilly music was <u>like country music with a faster pace</u>. The speaker also talks about <u>rockabilly artists like Wanda Jackson being the early icons of Rock 'n' Roll</u>.

The lecture challenges the reading <u>by saying Rock 'n' Roll music came from rockabilly music, not the blues</u>.

Check-up

Page 140

1. massive   2. bilingual   3. mix
4. hits   5. translate   6. language

[Review 2]

Independent 1

Page 141

Sample Answer 1

Disagree

Topic: Money <u>cannot</u> buy happiness.
A. <u>The most important things in life are personal relationships</u>.
  1. <u>If I didn't have family and friends, I would be miserable</u>.
  2. <u>It would be nice to have no debt but it does not make you happy—people do</u>.
B. <u>I would never want to be rich and alone</u>.
  1. <u>A woman won the lottery and moved into a new house by herself</u>.
  2. <u>The woman missed her friends and was lonely</u>.
Conclusion: For these reasons, I <u>would rather be happy than rich</u>.

I think that money <u>cannot</u> buy happiness. I think this because <u>the most important things in life are personal relationships</u>. For example, <u>if I didn't have family and friends, I would be miserable. It would be nice to have no debt, but it does not make you happy—people do</u>. In addition, <u>I would never want to be rich and alone</u>.

For instance, <u>a woman, who my mom knew, won the lottery. The first thing she did was move into a new house in a new place, by herself. She missed having friends around who she could trust. She was very lonely</u>. It is for these reasons that I <u>would rather be happy than rich</u>.

Sample Answer 2

Agree

Topic: Money <u>can</u> buy happiness.
A. <u>Spending money on things you love makes you happy</u>.
   1. <u>I bought a big screen TV, which made me very happy</u>.
   2. <u>When money is scarce, I experience constant anxiety</u>.
B. <u>I admire people with a lot of money</u>.
   1. <u>If I were rich, I could retire at a young age</u>.
   2. <u>I could live off my assets for the rest of my life</u>.
Conclusion: For these reasons, I <u>think money is the key to happiness</u>.

I think that money <u>can</u> buy happiness. I think this because <u>spending money on things you love makes you happy</u>. For example, <u>last week I bought a big screen TV, which made me very happy. When money is scarce, I experience constant anxiety. However, when there is money in my bank account, I have nothing to worry about</u>. In addition, <u>I admire people with a lot of money. Their lifestyle appeals to me</u>. For instance, <u>I don't like to work. If I were rich, I could retire at a young age. Then I could live off my assets for the rest of my life</u>. It is for these reasons that I <u>think money is the key to happiness</u>.

Integrated 1

Page 142

Step 1

Reading

Main idea: The ATM made it easier <u>to spend money</u>
Key points:
- Before ATMs, we had to go to the <u>bank to get money</u>
- ATMs made it easy to get money <u>anytime, anywhere</u>
- People now pay with <u>credit cards</u>
- Soon, we won't need <u>cash at all</u>

Lecture

Main idea: Technology has changed how we <u>use money</u>
Key points:
- Not many people carry cash <u>in the US</u>
- We may not need to take cash out or use <u>credit cards</u>
- Some countries use <u>cell phones to pay for things</u>

Page 143

Step 3

Topic: The reading and the lecture talks about how technologies have changed how we use money.
A. The reading talks about
   1. how ATMs made spending <u>money easier</u>
     • Before ATMs, you had to <u>go to the bank to get money</u>
   2. how we might <u>never need cash</u>
B. The lecture says
   1. very few people carry a lot of <u>cash with them in the US</u>
   2. we may not need cash or <u>credit cards</u>
     • Some countries already use <u>their cell phones</u>.
     • It will be very easy to <u>pay for things</u>.
Conclusion: The lecture supports the passage by giving an example of how ATMs are useful and how we might not need cash in the future.

Step 4

The reading and the lecture talk about how <u>technologies have changed how we use money</u>. The reading talks about <u>how ATMs made spending money easier</u>. Before ATMs, you <u>had to go to the bank to get money</u>. The author goes on to say that, we <u>might never need cash</u>.

The lecture supports this by talking about how very few people <u>carry lots of cash with them in the US</u>. The speaker discusses how we may not <u>need cash or credit cards</u>. Some countries already <u>use their cell phones to pay for things. This means it will be very easy to pay for things</u>.

The lecture supports the passage by <u>giving an example of how ATMs are useful and how we might not need cash anymore at all</u>.

Integrated 2

Page 144

Step 1

Reading

Main idea: The charts show the popularity of <u>songs</u>
Key points:
- New songs are <u>ranked</u>
- Any genre of music can be featured but <u>most of it is pop music</u>
- Certain pop icons <u>always appear on the charts</u>

Lecture

Main idea: People should not just listen to <u>music that is on the charts</u>

Key points:
- Only pop music is <u>featured on the charts</u>
- If the artist is not famous or doesn't have a lot of money, then they won't <u>be on the charts</u>
- The charts make it difficult for unknown <u>artists to become known</u>

Page 145

Step 3

Topic: The reading and the lecture are about music charts.

A. The reading says the charts are a tool to show <u>the popularity of songs</u>.
  1. Most music on the charts is <u>pop music</u>.
  2. Other genres might be <u>featured as well</u>.

B. The lecture says that people <u>should not just listen to music that is on the charts</u>.
  1. If the artist is not famous or rich, <u>then they won't be on the charts</u>.
  2. The charts make it difficult <u>for unknown artists</u>.

Conclusion: They differ mainly because the lecture talks about how the charts make it difficult for other types of music and artists to be heard.

Step 4

The reading and the lecture are about <u>music charts</u>. They are a tool the music industry uses to <u>show the popularity of songs</u>. It goes on to explain that most music <u>on the charts is pop music</u>. However, other genres might be <u>featured as well</u>.

The lecture says that <u>some people only listen to music that is on the charts</u>. This is bad because <u>if the artist is not famous or rich, they might not be on the charts</u>. The speaker goes on to say that, <u>the charts make it difficult for unknown artists to become known</u>.

The reading and the lecture differ <u>mainly because the lecture talks about how the charts make it difficult for other types of music and artists to be heard</u>.

Page 146

Sample Answer 1
Agree

Topic: The best size school to go to is <u>a big one</u>.
A. <u>Bigger schools have more resources</u>.
  1. <u>A big library</u>.
  2. <u>The most advanced technology</u>.
B. <u>Bigger schools have better professors</u>.
  1. <u>The professors are well known in their fields</u>.
  2. <u>The professors are of high quality</u>.
Conclusion: I think <u>big schools are better</u>.

I think the best size school to go to is <u>a big one</u>. I think this because <u>big schools have more resources such as books, technology and professors</u>. For example, <u>a big school will have a big library. It will also have the most advanced technology</u>. Furthermore, <u>they have better professors</u>. I think this because <u>the professors are typically more well known within their fields. Therefore, they are of high quality</u>. In conclusion, I think <u>big schools offer the best education to students because of the abundance of resources they have on hand and because of the quality of professors they employ</u>.

Sample Answer 2
Disagree

Topic: The best size school to go to is <u>a small one</u>.
A. <u>You can get a better education</u>.
  1. <u>Small schools have smaller classes</u>.
  2. <u>Smaller classes are a better learning environment</u>.
B. <u>You are treated as an individual</u>.
  1. <u>Gives more opportunity for participation</u>
  2. <u>Can become more involved with professors</u>
Conclusion: I think <u>small schools are better</u>.

I think the best size school to go to is <u>a small one</u>. I think this because <u>small schools let you get a better education</u>. For example, <u>they have smaller class sizes. This makes a better learning environment</u>. Furthermore, <u>it will let students be treated as individuals. It will give students more of an opportunity to take part in discussions</u>. I think this because <u>a class of twelve students is a better learning environment than one with a hundred and twenty students. Also, students can be more involved with their professors</u>. In conclusion, I think <u>small schools offer the best education to students because of the close-knit community of students and professors</u>.

Answer Key

Worksheets Answer Key

[Unit 1]

Part A

1. (✓)   2. (✗)
3. (✓)   4. (✗)
5. (✗)   6. (✓)
7. (✓)   8. (✗)

Part B

1. adopted   2. legal
3. permitted   4. vote
5. tax   6. seemingly
7. afford   8. future

Part C

1. I permit my sister to use my computer for her homework.
2. My dad visits my grandma every week.
3. They swam across the pool three times.
4. We offered some money to the poor man.
5. Mark likes sleeping in the afternoon.

[Unit 2]

Part A

1. (✗)   2. (✓)
3. (✓)   4. (✗)
5. (✓)   6. (✓)
7. (✗)   8. (✓)
9. (✗)   10. (✗)

Part B

1. was   2. like
3. look   4. seems
5. imitates   6. shows
7. is   8. appreciate
9. find   10. uses

Part C

1. The towns are very large.
2. The dogs take a nap every afternoon.
3. The shirts look like they're from a different era.

[Unit 3]

Part A

1. However   2. also
3. Therefore   4. However
5. Therefore   6. However

Part B

1. D   2. A
3. F   4. C
5. E   6. B

Part C

1. I like short hair. However, my friend thinks it is ugly.
2. I enjoy reading mystery novels. I also enjoy reading comic books.
3. My brother kept teasing me. Therefore, I hit him.

[Unit 4]

Part A

1. obligation   2. advice
3. expectation   4. certainty
5. obligation   6. advice
7. obligation   8. certainty

Part B

1. Should I order pizza or spaghetti?
2. He should get a prism.
3. You must be nervous.
4. You must not mumble during the interview.
5. You should scatter these seeds.
6. It should start raining soon.

[Unit 5]

Part A

1. N   2. V
3. N   4. V
5. V   6. N
7. N   8. N

Part B

1. advice
2. production
3. decide
4. consider
5. advised
6. produces
7. consideration
8. decisions

Part C

1. My teacher's help made me understand math better.
2. My parents' advice was to major in English literature at university.
3. The cost of the sports car is too much for my budget.

[Unit 6]

Part A

1. explains
2. notes
3. states
4. claim
5. emphasizes
6. challenges

Part B

1. The writer suggests that student evaluations would allow teachers to know how much they are appreciated.
2. The lecturer refutes Dr. Johnson's research, and claims that her own research resulted in the only correct data.

[Unit 7]

Part A

1. Pr
2. Pa
3. Pr
4. Id
5. Pr
6. Pa

Part B

1. D
2. C
3. F
4. E
5. B
6. A

Part C

1. I will meet my friends for dinner.
2. I think it will be a beautiful day.

[Unit 8]

Part A

1. fun
2. mistakes
3. profits
4. a break
5. dinner
6. notes

Part B

1. take risks
2. has fun
3. take action
4. take time
5. has a headache
6. made a decision

Part C

1. I would have dinner with the President of the United States because we would get to eat in the White House.
2. I made an embarrassing mistake when I called my girlfriend the wrong name. She got really angry at me.
3. The biggest risk I ever took was when I traveled to Europe by myself.

[Unit 9]

Part A

1. (✗)
2. (✓)
3. (✓)
4. (✗)
5. (✓)
6. (✓)

Part B

1. but
2. so
3. or
4. and
5. but
6. so

Part C

1. I will see a concert, and I will cook dinner for my family.
2. I love to eat spicy food, but my parents don't like it.
3. I am studying English so I can get a good job, and so I can travel around the world.

Answer Key

[Unit 10]

Part A

1. Second,
2. Moreover,
3. Lastly,
4. In addition,
5. Furthermore, AND Finally,

Part B

(B) Third/Thirdly/Finally
(D) Second/Secondly/Next
(F) First/To begin/In the first place

Order: E, C, F, A, D, G, B

[Unit 11]

Part A

1. (✓)
2. (✗)
3. (✓)
4. (✓)
5. (✓)
6. (✗)
7. (✗)
8. (✓)

Part B

1. wear away
2. exist
3. used to help
4. used to wash AND use
5. saw
6. use to be

Part C

1. I didn't use to like mushrooms, but I love to eat them now
2. I used to love playing in the dirt, but I don't like it anymore.
3. I usually watch a movie and stay at home.

[Unit 12]

Part A

1. After
2. Then
3. Before
4. Third
5. During
6. First AND Last

Part B

1. Before that , After that
   Frederick Douglass wrote an important autobiography. After that, his words helped end slavery in the US. Before that, he escaped slavery.

2. Second, First, Last, Third
   First, slavery began in the US in the 1600s.
   Second, it was banned in 1865.
   Third, unfair Jim Crow laws were made in the Southern US.
   Last, African Americans gained more equality in the 1900s.